Warriors of Ethiopia

Ethiopian National Missionaries —
Heroes of the Gospel in the Omo River Valley

BY DICK MCLELLAN

ॐ ❀ ॐ

Chosen men who were Warriors
　　　　　　　　　　1 Kings 12:21

WARRIORS OF ETHIOPIA:
Ethiopian National Missionaries —
Heroes of the Gospel in the Omo River Valley
By Dick McLellan

All proceeds from the sale of Warriors of Ethiopia will support the work of evangelists and the Ethiopian Church.

Copyright © 2006 Richard J McLellan

First Published November 2006, 2007, 2008, 2011 & 2012 (Kingsgrove Press); Reprinted 2013 (Lost Coin); Reprinted eBook format 2020 (Cherrymetal); Reprinted 2025 (InghamSpark)

Front Cover Photo: Hamar Warrior at Buska in Omo Valley — all photographs by Dick and John McLellan

This book was revised in 2025 by Dick and John McLellan with minor alterations to the layout, text and the inclusion of some new photographs. However, it remains substantially the same as text printed in 2006 and that of the audio version readings by the author, Dick McLellan, as produced by Global Recordings Network.

ISBN 978-1-7643474-3-3 (paperback)

ISBN 978-1-7643474-1-9 (hardcover)

Bible Verses: unless otherwise stated, Scripture verses are rough translations or paraphrases of the Ethiopian Bible that is similar to the New King James Version.

All rights reserved. No part of this publication may be reproduced, stored in a retrieval system or transmitted, in any form or by any means, electronic, mechanical, photocopying, scanning, recording or any other — except for brief quotations in printed reviews, without the prior written permission of the publisher.

Emails for Contact: *Light4Ethiopia@gmail.com* or *Light4Ethiopia@outcome.com*

DEDICATION

To Vida, my wonderful wife, mother of our four children, missionary, nurse, who since 1954 has served the Lord with me in SIM and GR/LRI, sometimes in isolated, lonely places among animistic tribes, has shared in the joys and persevered in the sorrows of missions, in difficult situations and trials and has always fully supported me in my many ministry journeys.

&

To missionary wives, both expatriate and Ethiopian, whom we love, respect and honour, whom it was our privilege to know and serve with and to whom we owe so much. Without the wives, not much would have been done.

&

To the memory of the 'Running Preachers,' mainly unknown or forgotten today, but loved and respected in the history of the Wolaitta Church — the small band who ran through the dark nights, risking their lives to take the Gospel of Christ to hundreds of Wolaitta villages during the Second World War. Only four survived the war. and only one is still alive.

THANKS

To Lesley, Margaret, Judy, Vida, Mavis, Pearl, John, Keith, Chris and many others who gave and many others who gave their time to transcribe recordings, check the drafts, give advice, make corrections, do the layout, design and drawings or help with computer problems; and to many friends who prayed, encouraged me to write and who prayerfully supported Vida and me through the years. The Lord will bless and reward your faithfulness.

☯☪

FORWARD

More than half a century ago God called a young man to leave home in Australia for ministry in Ethiopia. Hardly knowing where it would take him he could not have imagined the journey would bring him into contact with an unusual group of men who would become his companions in the greatest of all enterprises.

Halfway around the globe in Ethiopia, the Lord was calling other men for His purposes. Most of them were farmers from several tribes as culturally and linguistically different from one another as the Irish are from the Italians. One thing they shared in common: a love for the Lord Jesus. It was He who had redeemed them from fear of death, from tormenting evil spirits and from the never-satisfied demands of the witchdoctors. Jesus Christ was their Liberator, their Chief. They would serve Him to the ends of the earth, even to death, a resolve that would be tested often in the coming years.

Eventually the lives and callings of the young Australian, Dick McLellan, and the intrepid company of farmer-evangelists would intersect. The consequence would be more than cross-cultural companionship, more than mutual encouragement; it would result in taking the gospel into previously inaccessible regions, to people so fierce they would not hesitate to kill an outsider. It was in this way the gospel would penetrate the darkness that had gripped the peoples in and around the Omo Valley for countless centuries.

This little book is about that intersection between the missionary and those Ethiopian evangelists. It is a brief record of some of these chosen men of God who left their fields, the familiarity of their culture, the security of their families and who, with Bible and water bottle in hand and confidence in their Saviour, took the message of Christ Jesus over the mountain ranges and beyond the rivers to those who had never heard of Him. It is about their conviction that people without Christ are truly and eternally lost. It is about their dedication to the One who had said, *"Go! I'll be with you."*

And they went. Today, through the sacrifices and sufferings of men like these, there are thousands of churches throughout the mountains of southern Ethiopia.

No less than the men whose stories he tells is Dick McLellan a remarkable man of God. By the time I arrived in Ethiopia in 1967, Dick had already been roaming the hills and valleys with many of Ethiopia's 'warriors' for a dozen years. It was principally from him that I, as a young missionary, learned to love these men and to serve alongside several of them. The blessing to me has been priceless.

When we stand before the Lord on that eternal day and He rewards the faithfulness of His servants, I do not doubt that far ahead in the line will be these men receiving a loving *"Well done!"* from their Chief. As for me, hearing these stories again, reminds me of how privileged some of us have been in knowing these ordinary men by whom God has been pleased through the 'foolishness' of what they preached to save those many who believed their message of new life in Christ.

Bark Fahnestock:
Tikempt Ishet,
Ethiopia
2006

CONTENTS

Introduction: *Untying Some Knots*

1.	Dafarasha: *Slavery and Redemption*	...	1
2.	Mahae: *A Pioneer Missionary*	...	15
3.	Dango: *A Bible at Any Price*	...	25
4.	Kebba: *The Least I Can Do*	...	32
5.	Nana: *The Invisible Man*	...	38
6.	Laliso: *The Gold Leaves*	...	47
7.	Onisa & Gebre: *A Rumour from the Lord*	...	53
8.	Tekka: *Angels Unaware*	...	63
9.	Waja: *The Prisoner of the Lord*	...	71
10.	Desalegn: *Adopted for Life*	...	80
	Photographs	...	87
11.	Gwobata: *The Cripple's Dream*	...	103
12.	Tekka: *A Martyr for Christ*	...	112
13.	Jemari: *Culture Shock and Courage*	...	127
14.	Nana: *An Unusual Prayer*	...	135
15.	Desta: *Names are Important*	...	142

CONTENTS

16.	Fanta: *An Unlikely Candidate*	…	146
17.	Tassew: *Tortured for Christ*	…	151
18.	Aldabo: *The Crooked Tree*	…	158
19.	Aldabo: *The Man at the Funeral*	…	168
20.	Ekaso: *Prayer Warfare*	…	174
21.	Bekele: *Brigands and Blessings*	…	182
22.	Tumoli: *The Gangster*	…	189
23.	Tona: *Spiritual Warfare*	…	197
24.	Birhanu: *Special Babies*	…	207
25.	Matewos: *Along Unfamiliar Paths*	…	213
25.	Matewos: *The Mediator*	…	218
27.	Yohannis: *Singing for Jesus*	…	224
28.	Belaynesh: *A Mother to Me Also*	…	233
29.	Rebecca: *Three Requests*	…	239
	A Final Word: *Living Sacrifices*	…	245

INTRODUCTION
Untying Some Knots

☙ ✿ ❧

We were standing on a ridge near the end of the Ometi range of mountains. The vast Omo River Valley lay before us. Thousands of feet below, the hot plains of southern Ethiopia shimmered in the sun. A thick smoky haze hung over the lowlands where a whirlwind sucked dust, grass and leaves up into the air. The grass-thatched huts of a hundred villages blended into the brown elephant grass and acacia trees to be mostly hidden from view.

It was the people that we sought, the people of the valley. There is a multitude of tribes there: Aari, Bunna, Hamar, Dassanech, Malae, Karo, Nyangatom, Tsemai, Erebori, Dimae, Mursi and the much-feared Bodi. Many others that we didn't know about were there too. Some were brown, some black. Tall Nilotic cattle herders and short peasant farmers; many great hunters and all fierce warriors. They were all down there, waiting. Like so many generations before them, they were all there in spiritual darkness, waiting. They had waited so long for messengers to bring them the Gospel of Jesus Christ. Too long!

Buzdi, the young man beside me, pointed with his chin to the sun shining on the water of the great Omo River. He showed me where other streams flowed into the Omo from the mountains further west. Closer, we saw men with their oxen and wooden ploughs on the hilly slopes below us. Others worked with their digging sticks on the steeper mountainsides. They were preparing ground for the rains that were to come.

We prayed together there on the mountain. Buzdi thanked God for the evangelist who walked 200 kilometres into his area, had told him of Christ and led him to the Saviour. I thanked the Lord for the lady who started a little Sunday School and led me to Christ.

We prayed for the lost tribes. With their strange languages and cruel customs, they waited to be told of freedom, of eternal life. I wondered how to reach them. Who could go to all these tribes, to all those villages, to all the different languages? Buzdi poured out his heart to God, with tears running down his dusty face.

Sweeping his arm over the valley, he cried, "O Lord, they are tied in Satan's rope and can't get free. Please send someone to untie the knots."

This book is a record of how God answered that earnest prayer and some of the Ethiopian national missionaries, the evangelists the Lord used to plant His church there. It names just a few of the special men, the spiritual warriors, who hazarded their lives for Jesus' sake in the mountains and on the plains of the Omo River Valley.

They went to untie some of the knots in Satan's rope.

Dick McLellan

1
DAFARASHA
Slavery and Redemption

೦ಜ✿ৡ

You are in Christ Jesus who became for us, our righteousness, and sanctification and redemption.
                                              1 Corinthians 1:30

Therefore you are no longer a slave, but a son, and if a son, then also an heir of God through Christ.
                                              Galatians 4:7

The whole Bible class suddenly exploded! "That is him! That is him! That is his story! That is Dafarasha!" they shouted excitedly. They pointed with their chins and waved their hands to indicate the older, black man sitting by the window of the small classroom. Dafarasha was quiet and shy and much embarrassed to be the centre of attention.

೦ಜৡ

"Dafarasha, get up! Up and run! The slave traders are here! Quickly! Run to the forest and hide. Now! Run!" His mother grabbed her son off the mat on the dirt floor. She pushed the still groggy lad out the door. The boy gasped at the pandemonium in the village. Terrified people were running in all directions. Armed men with whips and ropes were chasing them. Here and there struggles took place as the captured ones were subdued and tied up. A gunshot sounded nearby and the distress cry echoed across the valley. "Run and hide!" his mother shouted again.

Dafarasha was gripped with a terrible fear. He seemed paralysed for a moment as frightening tales about slave traders filled his mind. Some years earlier Arab slave traders came and carried off some of his relatives. In blind panic he ran through the garden. He ran through the corn stalks, under the coffee trees and around the *inset* ~ false banana or plantain trees. Flight was his only thought as he raced into the bushes and headed for the forest. He heard the cries of others running, but his only desire was to escape. His stubby legs propelled him up the hillside and he gasped for breath.

He didn't quite make it! Two men cut off his escape. They threw him on the ground and quickly tied his arms behind him and hobbled his ankles. Just eight years old, the stocky lad cried out for his mother. His father and younger brother escaped capture because they were away hunting in the forest and his mother was left because she was in late pregnancy.

ଔଓ

Dafarasha belonged to the Oyda tribe who lived in the deep valleys and the fertile Ometi mountains in southern Ethiopia. Groups of Oyda men turn over the ground on the steep mountain slopes with their long digging sticks to plant sweet potatoes and corn. They made wooden traps to capture the leopards and servile cats in the forests where coffee grew wild. They hung their bark beehives high in the forest trees for a good supply of honey. The quality of the honey was well known and had a ready market. The hunters shot their arrows up into the trees to bring down the lovely black and white colobus monkeys. The skins were valuable as they were highly prized by the Amhara tribe for floor mats and wall decorations.

The very black Oyda people were stockily built and wonderfully strong. The men carried heavy loads on their heads and the women across their lower backs. Many Oyda women wore skirts made from the bark of trees. Many men had just a loin skin or a wrap-around animal skin. They were despised by the lighter skinned tribes of the north who ruled over them for generations, who used and abused them, but valued them highly as slaves and household servants. Arab slave traders had, through the years, captured many Oyda people, marching them off in chains to distant provinces or to sell to Yemen, Saudi Arabia and the Gulf States.

The Oyda people, like the neighbouring Aari, Malae, Basketo and Galila tribes, lived their lives in fear. Fear of slave traders. Fear of the harsh demands of their rulers. Fear of their many witchdoctors who perpetuate the fear by consulting demonic powers, using poisons and imposing curses. The *budda* ~ 'evil eye' of the witchdoctors caused many to quake in terror. Some just give up all hope and literally died of fright. Or, they came crawling on their stomachs, bringing a gift of an animal and begging release from the curse. This 'peace offering' often put the person into huge debt that only increased their burden.

The witchdoctors had always to be asked for their permission when the farmers could plough or dig the soil, to plant a crop or to harvest it. They predicted the future and could always find an excuse for the failure of any of their prophecies — usually some innocent person being pointed out as the guilty offender.

However, the Oyda peoples' greatest fear was death itself — the unknown. That great fear held them in bondage all their lives. That fear of the unknown, instilled from birth, had given them a multitude of taboos and restrictions. Only the men could sit on a stool; the women always on the floor. Their houses were different too. The round bamboo huts, thatched with grass, had no centre pole to support the roof. When a pregnant woman commenced labour, she hurried alone into the forest or among the false banana trees in the garden. No one went to help her until the cry of the baby was heard. If she had difficulty, there was no one to help. If she died, she died there alone.

Hearing certain birdcalls while on a journey were bad omens and sent the traveller scurrying home in fear, their trip forgotten for that day. Even moving shadows of certain trees, the moaning sound of wind through the trees, some cloud formations and certainly the rainbows were all objects of fear. Dark nights especially were to be feared and the Oyda people locked themselves and their animals inside until daybreak.

ೞ

Dafarasha was soon chained in a long line of captives. They were driven over the infamous slave trails across the mountains. The slave traders' whips cracked unmercifully whenever the line slowed down or hesitated to cross the rivers. Days and weeks went by as more young captives were added to the scores already taken. They were from many different tribes and spoke a dozen different languages. The slave traders stole cattle and grain along the way so there always was plenty of food to keep the slaves in good condition. The captives carried the food to the next resting place, usually by a spring or at a river.

To young Dafarasha, the slave trails seemed endless and he lost track of the days. He was exhausted at the end of each day. At night he cried himself to sleep, but there was nobody to comfort him. At long last they reached a town in northern Ethiopia that had a large open-air market. Here the slaves were sold, often singly or in small groups. One large group was marched off towards the Red Sea coast to be shipped off to Saudi Arabia.

Dafarasha was fortunate to be sold to a rich Amhara landowner who already had several other slaves. He quickly learned enough of his master's language to obey orders.

Often he was abused and beaten when he made mistakes. Never once was he called by his name, but answered to "*Bariya* ~ Slave" or "*Shankilla* ~ Negro." The other slaves even made him wash their feet at night. He was a slave of slaves! From first light of dawn until sometimes late at night Dafarasha was kept in bondage, working hard. He had no rights. He could not protest about the unfair treatment meted out to him. He was fed on leftover food and often was hungry. Every night his foot was locked in a chain.

The weeks and months went slowly by Dafarasha grew bigger and stronger from the hard work in the fields, from carrying heavy loads on his head, bringing wood for the fires, water from the spring and grass for the animals. He became a valued and reliable servant for his master and he never caused any trouble. But, he never forgot his home and family away somewhere in the south.

෴

Six long years went by before his chance came. One night, after a bout of heavy drinking, his master forgot to attach the chain around Dafarasha's ankle. At midnight, Dafarasha escaped. Quietly creeping out of the house, the boy started to run — and run — and run!

Wearing only a pair of ragged shorts and a thin cloth that he wrapped around himself at night, Dafarasha ran for hours. He wanted to put as much distance behind him as possible. He imagined the consternation and anger when in the morning it was discovered that he had fled. He knew the landowner would send men after him. They would all be seeking the reward offered and his owner would afflict terrible punishment that would leave him scarred for life.

Dafarasha tried to blot out the fear that gripped him. He tried to think only of home, family and safety back in Oyda country. So he kept running all night. At dawn he found a ravine with water and lots of rocks and thick bushes for a hiding place. It was a long way from the road or any village. Exhausted, he drank some water and slept for a while. It was hard to sleep. He was hungry, thirsty and fearful that he would be found. He remained in hiding all day. Every moment he expected to hear voices and dogs barking, but it remained quiet. Dafarasha wondered if the pursuers had gone a different way. Would they stay on the road and try and cut him off at the Blue Nile River. He knew there was only the one bridge where he could safely cross over the river.

As soon as it was dark, Dafarasha had a long drink and started running again. Sometimes he fell over logs or rocks and was scratched and bruised. But, he kept going all night. Then he found another hiding place and remained there all that day. Each following day he hid himself and each night he ran. He ran south — always south. He found a few berries to eat and some wild honey. There were a few bananas in a gully and a couple of small corncobs left in a field. He grew much thinner, but he kept going — south — always south.

ඥෑ

Dafarasha finally arrived at the mighty Blue Nile River. The guard on bridge duty knew immediately that he was an escaped slave. A short black boy, obviously from the despised tribes in the south, fear in his eyes, hungry and desperate, with no money to pay the fee and only a few rags for clothes — he had to be a runaway slave. The guard had seen a few others through the years, but none as young as this one. The guard let him pass. He had no love for the slave traders. Anyway, it was rumoured that slavery was now illegal throughout Ethiopia. The guard gave the boy some thick bread to eat and a gourd of sour milk to drink. It tasted wonderful. Dafarasha wrapped some of the bread in the corner of his cloth to eat later. He thanked his benefactor and kept going south.

As he approached *Addis Ababa* ~ New Flower, the capital city, Dafarasha caught up with some traders with several dozen mules loaded with goods. They were heading south with rolls of cloth, clothes, beads, salt, sugar, axes and sickles that they would sell in the town markets along the way. The merchants were glad to let Dafarasha accompany them if he did his share of work. Work was something Dafarasha knew about! He helped to load the mules each morning and to adjust the loads during the day. He collected firewood at the campsite, brought water from the spring and helped to guard the mules at night.

He was travelling much more slowly now, but he felt safe with the traders. With their loaded animals they went no more than six hours a day. The traders fed him well and one day he heard the leader tell a man in a market who asked about him that Dafarasha was one of his team, a good, reliable worker. They gave him some clothes and looked after him during the weeks of travelling and trading. Dafarasha learned a lot from these men and when they stopped in Wolaitta, he was reluctant to say, "Goodbye." This was as far as they would go. They would quickly sell the last of their trading goods, buy coffee beans and spices and return the way they had come. The traders gave Dafarasha some new clothes, money and food. They wished him well, a safe journey and peace. They were sorry to see him go.

CG80

Dafarasha felt he was almost home! It was another 150 kilometres from Wolaitta to Gofa and Oyda country. He walked quickly, but carefully from village to village, asking the way and seeking any news of the slave traders. In a week he arrived home. At the last river he washed himself and his clothes. As he got closer he started to recognise familiar hills, trees and houses and he could no longer restrain himself. He burst into his village, racing flat out and shouting for his family!

O, the delight of that day!

The rejoicing that went on for days! His parents had long since given Dafarasha up for dead — lost forever. Now, after six years, their son was alive again — home! As they hugged and kissed him over and over, asking dozens of questions and laughing, crying and shouting, neighbours and family came running. Dafarasha saw his young brother Debelke and his sisters, friends — it was all too much. Overwhelmed, Dafarasha collapsed weeping on the ground. His parents carried him into the house.

It was several days before Dafarasha had recovered from the emotion of it all — the relief of again being free. Many Oyda people walked for hours just to see him, just to touch him. It was a miracle. Dafarasha was the only slave from their area ever to return. It was all so wonderful. Around the fires at night, Dafarasha's story was told and retold — lost, but found — dead, but alive again! But, it was a long time before Dafarasha could sleep easily at night.

The excitement settled down after a few weeks and Dafarasha slipped back into the Oyda way of life and culture. Work came easy, ploughing and digging, sowing, weeding and gathering, splitting wood, cutting grass and hunting in the forest. Four years rushed by and Dafarasha had become a strong, healthy young man. He was thinking about a girl to marry and as Oyda custom decreed, he would soon ask his parents to choose a wife for him. Dafarasha's entire world seemed at peace.

౷౸

Then it happened again! The unthinkable! A dawn raid, the gunshots, the running feet, the screams, the burning houses, people fleeing in every direction. This was to be the last raid by the Arab slave traders. Most people escaped, but like half a dozen other young fellows, Dafarasha was again run down and caught, tied up and marched off into slavery. Dafarasha was in utter despair as he again climbed the slave trails over the mountains.

All across the valley and along the mountain ridges, the Oyda distress cry rang out. It was repeated from village to village and men shouted the news from one hilltop to the next. Dafarasha was captured again! How could it be?

Awful fear gripped the hearts and minds of the superstitious Oyda people. What a hard taskmaster they had! *Shaitan* ~ Satan had kept the animistic Oyda tribe in darkness and poverty as they tried to keep up with the sacrifices and gifts demanded by the witchdoctors. But, what good did it do? Fear, the fear of the evil spirits, the unknown, the spirits of their ancestors and the fear of death, kept the people cowed and helpless.

When Dafarasha's brother Debelke heard what had happened while he was away hunting, he yelled a cry for help that echoed down the valley. Soon the whole neighbourhood gathered together. Debelke shouted that everyone must give everything they had to get Dafarasha back. Cattle, goats and chickens were rounded up and all the money from the people was collected. They persuaded their Amhara landowner to follow the trail through Gofa and catch up with the slaves. He was to take all the money they had collected and try to buy Dafarasha back. A group of the old men of the tribe followed with the animals.

About ten days later, it was a happy, triumphant group that returned. They had Dafarasha with them! It had taken all the money and animals they had, plus a lot of pleading and begging, but he was released. There was great rejoicing in all the Oyda country as the word spread that Dafarasha had been freed. The Government of Emperor Haile Selassie in Addis Ababa outlawed slavery in Ethiopia. There would be no more Arabs raiding the southern tribes. A few individuals, of different tribes, would still buy and sell people as 'servants,' but that too, would die out — in time.

ଓ୫୦

Dafarasha built a house for himself on the edge of the forest. He soon married — and the years passed by. Years later he heard of white foreigners coming to live near Bulki. It was said that they were teachers and had brought a 'new religion.' One day in Bulki market, Dafarasha saw the white man. He too was short, no taller than Dafarasha himself. Walter Ohman smiled and laughed a lot. Dafarasha heard him tell an Amhara man that the soap he had just bought could wash away the dirt, but only the blood of *Eyesus Kiristos* ~ Jesus Christ, God's Son, could wash away sin. He was intrigued, and with Debelke, followed the missionary to ask more about the One who could cleanse from sin.

It was all so strange, so different to anything they had heard before. And so hard for them to understand! The new words of love, forgiveness, repentance, faith and righteousness were all new concepts. Another missionary couple came to visit their village and Dafarasha and Debelke learned more about Christ from them. The brothers regularly visited the missionaries. Eventually they said they believed in Jesus and would follow Him.

But then, the Second World War swept all the missionaries away. There was no one to teach Dafarasha and his brother. It was fourteen more years before two Wolaitta evangelists, Mahae and Yohannis, came into Gofa. They travelled to Oyda territory, telling the story of Jesus over and over. And they found the untaught men who said they believed in Jesus. Mahae's young brother Daniel also became an evangelist and settled in the Oyda area.

☙❧

It was another eight years before we in SIM cleared all the hurdles of getting land to rent so we could establish a mission station at Minderae near the town of Bulki. Other people claimed the land where the pre-war station had been. Then came opposition from the Orthodox Church, red tape, delays and obstruction in Government offices, officials wanting bribes and all kinds of problems. It all caused us to have several fruitless trips from Bako by mule to try and obtain land. It was February 1959 when Vida and I arrived from Bako to work with the Wolaitta evangelists to bring the Gospel of Christ to the many tribes in Gofa Province.

Vida opened a Clinic and soon crowds of people came for medical help. She was kept busy all day as she treated their sicknesses and bandaged their wounds. The 'white lady in the white uniform,' as they called her, quickly earned a reputation for healing the sick, a powerful *hakim* ~ doctor. It seemed nearly everyone had malaria, tuberculosis, eye infections or a dozen other diseases. The new antibiotics she injected did wonders for the nasty ulcers that disfigured and crippled so many of them. While waiting their turn for treatment, the people listened to the Gospel records and heard the testimony of a young believer who helped Vida. These contacts in the Clinic led to open doors for the evangelists out in the villages. Soon *selot bet* ~ prayer houses were started in a score of villages where new believers gathered to learn about Christ and how they were to live as they 'walked the Jesus Road.'

☙❧

As soon as possible we started a Bible class for the chosen leaders of the many new churches. Three days a week the men of several tribes would study God's Word. The problems faced by the first Christians in Corinth, Athens and Philippi were similar to their own. Both the problems and the persecution! These new believers were just so excited and keen to learn. They lapped up the lessons and hurried home to share new truths with their congregations. Then they came back early for more!

There were no Scriptures in their own languages and all teaching had to be given in Amharic with interpretation into Gofa. They loved the Amharic Bible, but few were fluent in this language. There were all kinds of linguistic difficulties and often we laughed over hilarious misunderstandings and mistakes.

One day we were studying the first chapter of Paul's first letter to the Corinthians. It took some hours as we discussed the verse in Corinthians 1:30:

Christ Jesus who became for us wisdom from God, and righteousness and sanctification and redemption.

They seemed to understand, but if not fully comprehending it all, they delighted to claim more of the riches of God's grace to us in Jesus Christ.

However, when we read that Christ was our redemption, our ransom, they stumbled over the Amharic word '*bezza.*' Each one read it as *"bessa."* When I asked why they kept changing it, they said that they did not know what *bezza* meant, but they knew that a *bessa* was a small silver coin used before the war, but it had been out of circulation for a long time. They thought it showed that Christ, the Creator of the whole universe, had made Himself so small to come as a baby to live and die as a man, for us. It was a good thought, but not what Paul said to the early believers in Corinth!

I pointed with my chin out of the window towards the old slave trail over the nearby mountain. I imagined a slave, chained, helpless, having lost everything, going into bondage, mistreated, lost, but then miraculously bought back at a price, redeemed, made free. The ransom price was *bezza*. I said that was the price Jesus paid with His precious blood to redeem us, to free us from Satan's bondage.

Suddenly the whole class exploded! "That's him! That's his story! That's Dafarasha!" they shouted excitedly.

Pointing with their chins and waving their hands, they indicated the older, black man near the window of the small classroom. Dafarasha was quiet and shy and by now very embarrassed to be the centre of attention. But, as he told us his story, we all understood more fully, the wonder of the Gospel message. The Oyda people had waited for so long to hear of the One who came to die and, through His death, to:

> *free those who through fear of death lived all their lifetime in slavery.*
>
> Hebrews 2:14-15

EPILOGUE

Our old friend Dafarasha is now with the Lord he loved and served so faithfully. He was ridiculed, beaten and imprisoned for his faith in Christ, but he lived to see thousands of his tribe released from their bondage to Satan, sin and the fear of death. He saw many churches established among his people. Dafarasha's nephew Matewos, his brother Debelke's son, is now the pastor of the church in the village from which Dafarasha was twice taken as a slave. Let us, like Dafarasha, praise and thank God for Jesus Christ, Who paid the *Bezza* ~ Ransom for our sins.

2

MAHAE

A Pioneer Missionary
ଔ✿ଞ

In prison more frequently, flogged more severely, beaten with rods, once I was stoned, in journeys often, constantly on the move, in danger from rivers, from bandits, often without sleep, in hunger and thirst, cold and naked.
1 Corinthians 11:23 & 25-27

The first Ethiopian national missionary I ever met was Evangelist Mahae Choramo and he was in prison. It was very cold, early in the morning at 2,600 metres (8,500 feet) altitude, as I walked into Bulki town. A group of prisoners sat against a bamboo fence, trying to get warm in the sun. An armed guard stood watch over them. Mahae had shackles on his wrists and around his ankles. The chains rattled when he moved. His clothes were ripped and splattered with blood. His face was puffed up, his lip was split and he had lost quite a bit of skin from a savage beating he had endured overnight. Large drops of blood dripped onto his shoulder from an open head wound. There were cuts and bruises all over his body and he was obviously in a lot of pain.

And then Mahae tried to smile at me! He guessed that I was a missionary. Immediately something just 'clicked' between us; our spirits seemed to fuse into an instant bonding of fellowship, friendship and ministry that would last a lifetime. That recognition only happens between those who have the Spirit of the Lord Jesus Christ. In February 1955, I had been in Ethiopia for only six months and knew very little of the Amharic language. With Bill Carter from England, I was on my way to help build the SIM mission station at Bako that was to be a base for reaching many different tribal groups in the Omo River Valley with the Gospel.

A man told me Mahae's name and that he was an evangelist. He said that officials had Mahae beaten up because of his preaching. When I asked about Mahae's wounds, the prison guards were somewhat embarrassed. They quickly shuffled all the prisoners back into the filthy huts. There was just time for me to put my hands on his and give them a squeeze. From my pocket I gave him some painkillers and a couple of pieces of bread. I slipped a few dollars into his blood-soaked shirt pocket and said, "I'll pray for you." It was our first meeting, but it changed my life and helped shape my future ministry.

ଓଽଠ

This wasn't the first time Mahae had been incarcerated for preaching, nor would it be his last. Once, with him, I counted the number of times he had been arrested and imprisoned for the Gospel's sake. We counted twenty-seven times. Since then, he has been imprisoned at least six more times! Usually it was for a few weeks or months, sometimes longer. Once he spent five long years in Kucha prison. On the Kucha Mountain, a row of giant cedar trees that he planted, watered and cared for during those five years are still called 'Mahae's Cedars.' One time I heard Mahae praise the Lord that he had been in every prison south of Soddo! Of course, it was not much of a disgrace to be imprisoned in Ethiopia, especially for Jesus!

Like all the Ethiopian evangelists, Mahae accepted persecution and suffering as a part of his ministry — inconvenient, difficult for his family, but necessary — a price to pay as an ambassador for Christ. He knew he was called to *"endure hardship as a good soldier of Jesus Christ."* Gladly he suffered the privations, the abuse, the beatings and the imprisonments for Christ. Being in gaol gave Mahae the opportunity to share the Good News with an attentive, captive audience. Many a believer has testified that he came to Christ after heard the Gospel from an evangelist while in prison.

༅༅

A few years after our first meeting, Mahae and I stood together as prisoners in the Bulki courtroom. Three angry judges, an even angrier priest from the Ethiopian Orthodox Church, several court officials and the police prosecutor all shouted at us together.

I had spent a couple of hours in the government compound where the Governor's office, the Courts, the Tax office and the Police Station were located. A great wave of persecution was sweeping over Gofa Province. Church buildings were burnt down, the Christians' houses looted and their animals stolen. Some Christians had been killed. I presented a petition to the Governor about the harsh treatment being meted out to the evangelists in Bulki prison. After months, they had not even been charged with any crime, but were being abused by the guards at Bulki prison who had a well-earned reputation for their brutality and corruption. They augmented their low wages by extorting money from the families of the prisoners with threats of more beatings. The forty-one Wolaitta evangelists and a dozen elders were arrested at their monthly prayer and fellowship meeting. Savagely beaten and often denied food and medical attention, some were quite sick.

I received no help from Governor Kibret; only being told *"Ishi nega. ~* OK tomorrow." But then, a policeman had summoned me into the Police Commander's office. Colonel Bekele and the Governor always appeared friendly to me, but they supported the Orthodox priests in their persecution of the evangelical Christians. The Colonel was angry and felt insulted because his own personal bodyguard Tanga had become a believer, one of the despised 'Jesus People' and no longer took bribes or passed them on to his Commander! He had Tanga dismissed from the police service and imprisoned, in chains, for six months. As the police chief accompanied me out onto the veranda, in the distance we could hear a crowd singing.

As the sound came closer, we could hear the words:

"We follow Jesus Christ — we follow Him,
Creator of the world — we follow Him,
Jesus Christ the Lord — we follow Him,
Mighty Son of God — we follow Him,
Crucified on Calvary — we follow Him,
He died and rose again — we follow Him,
Now exalted in Heaven — we follow Him,
He is the only Saviour — we follow Him,
He is always with us — we follow Him,
All the way He leads us — we follow Him"

The song echoed up the street and through the town. It was a 'choir in chains' who shuffled along the winding track from the prison towards the courthouse. All fifty-three men had chains on their wrists and some also had shackles on their ankles. Many were in pain from infected sores caused by the rough chains, but they boldly sang to proclaim their allegiance to the Lord Jesus Christ. Mahae led the song that he made up as he went along. The other prisoners thundered out the refrain "we follow Him" at the end of each line.

These men had been in Bulki prison together for months, sharing the little amount of food brought to them. As 'prisoners on remand' they were not fed by the prison authorities, but had to survive on gifts of food brought by relatives and friends. Often they were hungry.

They now expected to receive a sentence for their faith in Christ. Once they were charged and sentenced, they would qualify for some food from the prison kitchen. This would relieve their families who were in great distress themselves because of the persecution raging through the villages of Gofa — wherever 'Jesus People' were to be found.

By the time the Christian group reached the government compound, they had gathered a large following of town people. Crowds of children ran to see the fun!

"They are more like conquerors than prisoners!" said an old man to his wife.

"Yes," she replied, "like an army on the march."

I had not heard that the Christians were to have a hearing in court that day. As they came through the gate and neared the courthouse, Mahae finished off the song with the usual "Forever and all eternity!" and his companions roared out "Forever we follow Jesus!"

Then Mahae saw me and shouted a greeting. He ignored the Police Commander! All the believers shouted greetings and banged their chains together. They surrounded me, shaking hands, laughing and rejoicing. In my heart I thanked God for such men, steadfast, faithful, bold.

The reunion didn't last long! Several policemen and the prison guards came running to drive the prisoners away. They arrested me, marched me into the court and charged me with "consorting with criminals" and "disturbing the peace." The evangelists were also crowded in for their trial and they lined up three deep along a side wall of the courtroom.

The main judge shouted angrily at me, "What were you doing among the prisoners?"

"I was greeting my friends," I replied, in what I hoped was a steady voice. I had never been in a court before and I was a bit apprehensive.

"It is forbidden to go among the criminals," said the second judge — I had not gone to them — they had come to me! The third judge consulted with the priest who sat on the bench behind the judges.

The main judge talked for a while to the others on the bench and then said to me, "You are not permitted to go among the prisoners, but because you don't know the law, we will be lenient. You must stay here until the court rises. Where will you stand?" There were no chairs in the court except on the judges' bench.

I looked around the packed courtroom. Spectators filled the doorways and windows and more wanted to crowd in. I said, "These men are my brothers in Christ. I will stand with them," and pushed through the crowd and stood near Mahae. I ignored the murmurs among the crowd and the obvious anger of the judges.

For the first time I saw an Ethiopian court in action! I stood silently listening to all kinds of lies being told as accusations were levelled against the Christians. Most charges were obviously false about "opposing the government," "not paying taxes" and "changing the peaceful customs of the people." It would have been laughable if it were not so serious!

I was amazed at the influence of the priest who gave instructions to the three judges! He became increasingly agitated and angry. He stood up, waved his whip and shouted at the prisoners, "You have changed your religion. You refuse to pay the priest's tax. You teach the people to be 'Jesus People' and not be Orthodox. You don't keep the Church Fasts."

The Christians were not even given an opportunity to reply to a score of accusations. To me, it all seemed so unfair! The police prosecutor kept asking for long sentences to be given the believers. The judges seemed especially furious that the Christians did not observe all the Orthodox fasts. It seemed they would rather the animistic tribal people remain as spirit worshippers than to become followers of Jesus Christ. The main judge again waved his whip at the believers and shouted, "Yes, we Orthodox fast, but you don't fast!"

Suddenly, next to me, Mahae spoke up, "But, we do fast."

"What? What? Who said that?" demanded the judge. Mahae stepped forward. Obviously he had rattled the judge! "You do fast? Truly, you do fast? What do you fast from? Meat? Milk? Eggs? Butter?" the judge shouted.

" No," Mahae replied loudly for all to hear, "We fast from SIN."

There was uproar in the court! The spectators exploded! They roared with laughter and clapped their hands.

The fifty-three believers laughed and banged their shackles together. "Yes," they shouted, "We do fast! We fast from SIN!"

Many of the guards and onlookers also laughed and whispered to each other that the judge had gotten his 'comeuppance' which he deserved. The hubbub vibrated around the court. The judges and the priest were so furious — almost beside themselves! They banged their sticks and whips on the bench while the guards outbid each other shouting: "QUIET! QUIET!" as they tried to restore order.

ଔଡ଼

Years later Mahae and I drove across the plains towards a solitary mountain in that part of the Omo Valley. It is called the 'Mountain of Darkness' and it is well named. There were stories that only witchdoctors went up the mountain and that once a year, all the witchdoctors gathered at the top to sacrifice a teenage girl to *Shaitan* ~ Satan. None of the people were allowed to graze their animals on the mountain or to cut grass or collect wood for their fires. It was a place filled with the powers of darkness and the people feared it greatly.

With us in the car was Petros Esa, a young Aari evangelist, his wife and two small children. Petros was the first Aari Christian to bring the Gospel to the Bunna tribe. Others would follow him in days to come. Mahae, Petros and I talked to the people in a village near Bori, not far from the Mountain of Darkness. They were glad to have 'the new teaching,' as they called it. Mahae had gathered the wood, grass and vines necessary to build a house and so Petros was able to locate with his family among the Bunna people. Several people said they wanted to hear the 'Jesus Story' and for their children to learn to read.

While in the village, we all took turns to share the Gospel of Christ. Near the edge of the village sat an elderly lady who listened eagerly. Very old and wrinkled, she was light brown in skin colour, very different from the darker black people around her. She had been captured as a small child by marauding warriors and had lived all her life as a slave. Abused and mistreated, it was the only life she knew. Now, almost naked, she sat and listened for the first time, to the message of God's love. As she listened intently, she made a small clay dish. Holding the clay in one hand and turning it round and round with the other, she fashioned it into a perfectly round dish. As she listened, sometimes asking questions, she forgot the continual motion, but spat on the clay to keep it moist. Soon it was shaped, moulded and ready to be fired along with the other pots for carrying water, boiling coffee or cooking food.

When I finished telling of God's Son coming from Heaven to die on the cross for our sins, the lady said, "That is wonderful news! But, is it true?" In their oral traditions, the people have hundreds of stories — of animals, insects, birds, heroic deeds, tribal wars, local fights and of strange people. Some of the stories are true, but many are just made up and false. Hence her question, "Is it true?" We assured her that it is true — God loves us and gave His Son Jesus to pay for our sin and to redeem us to live with Him forever.

The old lady's face shone! After each story about the Lord Jesus, she said, "That is good, but is it true?" Finally Mahae and I slowly approached her on our knees — a sign of highest respect, usually reserved for women when they approach the Chief of the tribe. She, the slave and we missionaries, looked into each other's face. She put down the finished dish and said, "That is an amazing, wonderful story, but is it true?"

I touched her muddy hands and said, "My mother, it is true. It is all true. God the great Creator loves us so much. Jesus came to redeem us from sin and bring us out of the darkness so we can live in the light with Him." Mahae also assured her that the message is true, that Jesus saves from sin and Satan's power.

The woman looked at us and slowly replied, "Yes, it must be true. It must be true. But, if it is true, why didn't you come before and tell us?" Tears stung my eyes at her question and I had to turn away. I wished there was a hole I could crawl into and hide! I felt ashamed that we, who had the Good News of salvation for so long, had not delivered it before. Mahae and Petros earnestly explained how the woman could have forgiveness as a free gift and have a whole new life in Christ. In the days ahead, Petros and his wife would repeat the story over and over again. I wonder if she ever believed and accepted Christ.

CB&O

We had to go on our way, but Petros and his family stayed in the village near the Mountain of Darkness. It was a dangerous area and people were killed on the dusty trails that wound endlessly through the thorn trees, rocks and cactus plants. Some months later, Petros' wife became sick with malaria and Petros walked the three hours to the Mission Clinic for medicine. On the way home he was brutally murdered, his body mutilated and his watch and clothes stolen — a man's life for a cheap watch and a few ragged clothes. The circling vultures pointed the way to where Petros' body lay. Mahae and a missionary buried Petros in a lonely grave among the thorn trees. They piled up rocks so the hyenas could not disturb his body.

Some sixteen years later Mahae and I were again driving in that area. Mahae found Petros' grave. The stones were still piled up, but the wooden cross was gone that had said:

PETROS ESA
FAITHFUL UNTO DEATH

It had been eaten by termites long ago. The tree that marked the spot was also gone. But, the Mountain of Darkness still overlooks the great Omo River Valley with its many villages that wait for *"the Messenger of the Cross that cometh late."* But praise the Lord that around the mountain there are now many *selot bet* ~ prayer houses where Bunna people gather to sing praise to God Who sent the Light to shatter the darkness.

Mahae and I knelt in the dust by Petros' grave and prayed. We recommitted our lives to the Lord Jesus Christ and promised to be faithful in prayer and to go until every tribe and every village in the whole Omo River Valley was reached with the Gospel of His grace.

3
DANGO
A Bible at Any Price

In Me, you may have peace. In the world you will have tribulation, but be of good cheer; I have overcome the world.
John 16:33

His Word was in my heart like a burning fire shut up in my bones; I was weary of holding it back, and could not.
Jeremiah 20:9

"Do you have a Bible I can buy?"

The little man was only dressed in a tattered, old shirt and ragged shorts. Barefooted and dirty, he looked absolutely destitute. His hair was long and covered in lice. He certainly didn't look like he could afford to buy a Bible, or read it either. But then, I noticed he had open sores on his wrists and ankles.

Vida and I first met evangelist Dango when he came to our house on the mountains at Bulki. He came directly from the Bulki prison where he had spent several months. He had not even had time to wash or delouse himself after months in the filthy conditions of the prison. He had not even been home yet!

Dango was desperate to get himself another Bible. It would replace the one confiscated when he was arrested for preaching the Gospel. To Dango, the Bible was more important than food or clothes. He must have a Bible. "How can I preach the Good News without the Word of God in my hands?" he asked.

At least on this occasion, Dango wouldn't have to walk 300 kilometres (186 miles) to get one. He had done so before when he was imprisoned for preaching and they took his Bible. When we just presented him with a Bible as a gift, Dango was overwhelmed. He fell on his knees to praise God for the gift. His home church in Wolaitta sent him a few dollars support each month, but a Bible cost a whole month's allowance. And Dango had already lost three Bibles.

༄༅

With his wife, Tabita and their three little children, Dango had walked from Wolaitta into Gofa. He believed God had called him there to preach the Gospel of Christ. They loaded their few possessions on to a donkey for the long journey. The two smallest children also rode on top of the load. Mosquitoes, tsetse flies and flooded rivers were a nuisance and delayed the young couple for some time, but they did not stop them.

They settled on the edge of a village on the Gofa mountains. Dango obtained land and quickly built a small house with bamboo walls, dirt floor and grass thatch, like the people of the area. He planted a garden of sweet potatoes, corn and *insett* ~ plantain — the staple diet of the area. *Insett* is a type of banana that bears no fruit. The starchy core of the plant is eaten while the leaves are used to wrap things or as shelter from the heavy rains. The fibres are made into rope to tie loads and in building houses.

Soon Dango made trips to the surrounding villages, making friends and telling the story of Jesus over and over again. Seeking the lost. Challenging the powers of darkness. Preaching everywhere. Praying constantly. Always he carried his Bible. Some of the people seemed interested, but most were afraid of the anger of the local witchdoctor.

Tabita started reading classes for the boys and taught Bible stories to the village women and girls. She took an earthenware jar and boiled leaves from the coffee trees. She added spices, salt and butter and then called in her neighbours to share it. As they sat sipping the coffee, Tabita shared her testimony and explained the way of salvation. The women had never heard anything like this new teaching. It was hard to understand, but they kept coming.

ಬಿಂ

Dango travelled over the rocky mountain trails to Galila. He preached the Good News in many of the villages until an Orthodox priest had him arrested for "disturbing the peace." Dango spent the next three months in the local prison and had his money and his spare clothes stolen. And his Bible. He was severely beaten and threatened with harsher treatment, even death, if he ever returned to Galila. Then he was allowed to go.

Returning to his family, Dango told his wife, "I must go back to Wolaitta to get another Bible. It is my only authority. I must have God's Word in my hands when I preach." So again he walked the 150 kilometres (93 miles) and bought a Bible. It cost him a month's allowance. Then he walked 150 kilometres back. The journey took him nearly two weeks.

In their village and the nearby ones, Dango regularly gathered the people together and taught them from the Bible. More and more of them became interested in the message and they asked many questions. Dango also started to teach some teenage boys and young men to read.

The cold mountains of Wobhamar to the west called to Dango. A hard day's trek brought him into the centre of the Aari tribespeople. He preached in the villages and by the roadside. It was dangerous as he challenged the powers of darkness and pointed people to Jesus, the Light of the World. Dango was again arrested and badly whipped. He was abused and imprisoned for two months before he was chased out of the area. He again lost his clothes and money — and his Bible. Undaunted, Dango set out again, back to Wolaitta for another Bible.

When he arrived back again in Gofa, Dango was encouraged by the numbers of people asking about the 'Jesus Way.' Tabita's building of friendships among the neighbours was paying off. Within two years, more than 100 people turned to Christ. They openly renounced Satan and the worship of spirits. No longer did they consult any of the powerful witchdoctors who lived in the area. The first baptismal service in a nearby mountain stream saw dozens of people openly confess faith in Christ as Saviour and Lord.

ഃ⊙౪

That triggered violent opposition. The witchdoctors and the priests combined forces to persecute the 'Jesus People.' They gathered a mob of ruffians and attacked the new church during a Sunday morning service. They tied up Dango and the church elders, whipped them severely and dragged them off to prison.

The congregation was attacked with clubs, punched and kicked. Even the women and children were hurt and several had bones broken. Tabita tried to protect her children, but was beaten unconscious and trampled by the thugs. People ran in every direction trying to escape.

The church and Dango's house were burnt down and their gardens destroyed. The homes of a dozen new believers were also burnt down after the mob had looted all their possessions. All the cattle were driven away. The Christians were scattered far and wide.

The four church elders were cruelly beaten and then released. Like the previous times, Dango was not charged with any crime, but he was chained like a murderer and put in prison for nine months. He also lost his Bible.

Then Tabita died. This was mainly due to the savage beating she had received, followed by sickness and lack of food and medicine or proper care. Accompanied by an armed prison guard, Dango was released from the prison just for a day. He returned to the village to bury Tabita. All alone out on the windy hillside, Dango dug a grave and buried his wife. He mourned and prayed alone, watched by the guard who sat smoking nearby. Then Dango went back to prison. Only God heard the crying of Dango's heart.

Then more sorrow fell on the little evangelist. Within a month, two of his children also died of disease brought on by the harsh treatment and lack of food and care. Once again Dango was let out of prison for a day to conduct the funeral of his boys.

༄༅

Some months later rumours spread though the prison that some white people had come to Gofa and were building houses on the mountains near Bulki town. It was said that they were 'Jesus People' too and were preaching Good News in the villages. There was talk of schools being built. A medical clinic was opened and hundreds were going to the mission station at Minderae for help instead of to the witchdoctors. Word spread that priests and officials were angry about it and opposed their work.

When Dango was finally released from the prison he decided to go the long way home around the mountain so he could visit the missionaries. After giving us greetings, Dango asked, "Do you have a Bible that I can buy?" He received one as a gift.

Dango built another house for himself in the village. He gathered most of the scattered believers together and built another church too. He read his new Bible and preached and prayed. He also continued faithfully winning lost souls to Christ.

Then his eldest child, his only daughter, died suddenly one evening. Dango was devastated. He cried out to the Lord for help. Almost immediately two other evangelists, Nana and Amanta, arrived unexpectedly and they helped him through the crisis.

The next day I came on my mule and wept with the little man in his sorrow. His daughter was buried alongside her mother and brothers. For an hour we sat quietly together in the house. Then Dango said to me, "When I was in prison, the Lord was with me. When my wife died and all alone I had to bury her over there on the mountain, the Lord Jesus came to me. He came and comforted me and strengthened me. When my little boys died, again the Lord Jesus was with me. He supported me when I was so weak."

I replied, "The Lord Jesus always comes to His people in their times of need. He promised to be with us all the time. In the Gospel of John, Jesus said that in Him we might have peace. In the world we will have tribulation, but we rejoice that He has overcome the world."

"Yes, it is true," the little evangelist said, "He came to me when I was hurting so much. He said to me, 'Fear not, I am with you.'"

Outside, before I rode away, Dango swept his hand across the mountains towards Galila, Wobhamar, Aari, and then around towards Basketo, Mallo and Dimae. He said to me, "I hear God's Wind blowing on the mountains. That is why Satan is fighting so hard. People in darkness are calling out for the light. There probably will be much more suffering. But, the Bible is true and soon we will see Christ's church established all over Gofa."

"Amen, may it be so, for God's glory!" I replied.

EPILOGUE

The years have gone by and the Spirit of God has truly blown right across the mountains of Gofa. Across the mountains, down into the isolated valleys, along the mighty Omo River and over the other side too! Hundreds of churches have been established as thousands of people of the different tribes turned to Christ. As the fires burned brightly and the powers of darkness were shaken, chains of fear and bondage were broken. Animistic people lost their fear of evil spirits, witchdoctors, omens and death. The wailing has been replaced by praises and joyful worship of Jesus Christ. Waves of persecution also swept over the mountains. Witchdoctors and greedy priests, corrupt officials and communist cadres all opposed the Gospel of Christ and tried to destroy the church. Believers often lost their homes and possessions, many lost their freedom, some for up to five years — and some lost their lives.

But truly as Dango said, the Winds of God blew across the mountains and Christ's church was established. Praise the Lord it continues to grow. Dango lived long enough to see it all happen. In the last few years of his life, Dango lost his eyesight and could no longer read the Bible he loved so much. He made sure that every day one of the Christians who could read came to see him to read a chapter or two. This year, 2005, Dango went home to the Lord Jesus he loved so well.

4

KEBBA

The Least I Can Do

Others were tortured and refused to be released (at the price of denying heir faith), so they might be resurrected to a better life. Others had to suffer mocking and scourging, being chained and put in prison.

Hebrews 11:35-36

Vida saw the young fellow enter the mission compound and told me that a man was coming up the hill towards our mud house. She said that he looked very sad and distressed. When I saw it was Kebba, I wasn't surprised.

I went outside to meet him. Kebba stopped on the path and began to weep, tears running down his dusty face. I went up to him and took both of his hands in both of mine. And for a while I wept with him. After a few minutes Kebba stopped sobbing and quietened down. Then he looked up into my face and said, "John's father." (In that part of Ethiopia, it is the polite custom to call a friend after the name of his eldest child.) "John's father, my father died for Jesus Christ, didn't he?" he asked.

Kebba's father Minota was a wonderful man, a firm believer in the Lord Jesus Christ. He had welcomed the Wolaitta evangelists when they first brought the Good News of the Saviour to the Gofa mountains. Their message of repentance, forgiveness of sin, freedom from fear and God's gift of eternal life brought a ready response in Minota's heart. He was one of the first men in the area to renounce

Satan and follow Jesus. He found great joy in his new faith and gladly told his family and friends about the Lord. Soon his wife and Kebba accepted Christ too. Then some of their neighbours turned to the Saviour.

Minota gave a piece of his land to build a meeting place for the growing number of believers. All of the new Christians helped Minota and the evangelist Mahae build a small, round bamboo hut. They cut long grass to thatch the roof and made a bamboo door. The women plastered the dirt floor with cow manure to settle the dust and then the bamboo walls to keep out the icy cold winds. They called it their "*selot bet* ~ prayer house" and met there regularly to sing praises to the Lord Jesus and to pray together.

Minota especially enjoyed the monthly meetings of the evangelists and believers who gathered from different villages. They met each time in a different prayer house. Besides prayer and fellowship, they discussed problems that arose in the emerging churches. They shared stories of the suffering of new Christians and collected money to help those who lost their homes and possessions because of their faith in Christ. There was joy as more and more of the animistic people of Gofa turned to Christ, leaving the darkness and fear in which they had lived for so long.

ಬಐ

Some priests of the Orthodox Church soon became jealous and angry and stirred up persecution and suffering for the 'Jesus People,' as they called the followers of Christ. The Gofa people were animists who worshipped *Shaitan* ~ Satan, demons and the spirits of their ancestors, but they were also given names by the priests who then counted them as Orthodox. They were forced to pay a 'church tax' each year to the priests. In their exuberance as new believers, they refused to do this. The priests pressured the Governor and the Chief of Police to arrest the evangelists and expel them from the province. An order went out for all the 'Jesus People' to be arrested and for their prayer houses to be destroyed.

Most of the evangelists and many of the Gofa believers were arrested at one of their monthly gatherings. Minota was among them. With the police came a crowd of ruffians who took the opportunity to gather loot for themselves. Many believers were beaten when they protested. Some were punched and had their clothes torn from them. Others were whipped with an *alunga* ~ a hippopotamus-hide whip, resulting in long lacerations on their backs and legs. Then all the men were marched off to prison in Bulki town.

The wave of persecution swept right across Gofa Province and soon all twenty of the prayer houses were burnt down. The homes of many believers followed as unscrupulous officials and thieves pillaged their possessions. Their animals and food supplies were stolen and many families were driven off their land. Some were left destitute and endured great suffering as they sought shelter and food for their families. Some managed to find refuge with relatives and friends in other villages while some made leafy shelters in the bush. In the forest they collected berries and roots to eat. It was a whole year of suffering and great hardship for all those who dared to follow Jesus Christ. The exceptionally heavy rains that year and the cold winds increased their misery.

Reports of cruelty inflicted on the believers came in from distant villages. In one place three men were shot when they refused to recant their faith. In another, a young man was beaten to death. Believers were scattered in every direction. Some found refuge in caves or in the forest. Others went into distant provinces, but all remained faithful to the Lord.

༄༅

Every day in the notorious Bulki prison, the prison guards mocked and mistreated Minota and his friends. The poorly paid guards tried to supplement their wages by extracting bribes from all the new prisoners and their families. Many days the Christians had nothing to eat. Occasionally some of the other prisoners took pity on the believers and shared their small rations with them. Being kept for months as "prisoners on remand," but without being formally charged with any crime, they did not qualify to receive food from the prison kitchen. They had to be fed by their families from outside the gaol.

Minota was singled out by a couple of the guards for extra harsh treatment. They were angry with Minota's bold witness for Christ. At night he led the believers in songs of praise to the Lord. During the day he explained the way to Heaven to any of the prison inmates who would listen. He urged them, and even the prison guards, to repent of their sins and believe in Jesus Christ and be saved.

One guard was especially cruel in his treatment of the Christians. He viciously beat Minota with his rifle butt. He then crossed Minota's ankles and shackled them. He did the same with his wrists and then chained Minota's wrists to his ankles. The guard dragged Minota outside to the small fenced-off yard that was the open toilet area for all the prisoners. He tossed Minota into the filth and left him lying there in the muck. Then he threatened the other Christians that the same would happen to them unless they stopped singing and praying.

For nearly three weeks Minota lay in the chains out in the cold and rain. He was in agony, but suffered silently. Soon he had a bad cough and then a raging fever. He would have starved, but for his Christian friends who took him some food and water under the cover of darkness. Each night they covered him with a blanket.

Finally one day the guard who had chained Minota reported for work half drunk. He had Minota brought out of the toilet yard. The evangelists gently carried him into the courtyard of the prison. Minota was very weak, barely conscious and desperately sick. He urgently needed medical attention, but the guard did not care. "Now you will renounce your Jesus," the guard shouted at Minota, "Deny him and you can go free. You can go home."

Weakly Minota lifted his head to look at the guard. He had just enough strength to whisper, "I was lost in sin and darkness. I had no hope. Jesus, the Son of God, shed His blood on the cross and died for me. He saved me and gave me new life. I can never deny Him."

The guard exploded in anger and started kicking Minota with his heavy boots. All of the other prisoners, even the hardened criminals, started yelling out the distress cry. This cry brought more of the prison guards running and they dragged their companion away from stomping on Minota.

But it was too late.

Minota was dead. His broken body lay in the chains while guards and prisoners stared in horror. They had never seen anything like it.

The guards called the Warden of the prison from his house in the town and he soon arrived to take charge. He stopped the prayers and protests from the Christians and the death wail of the pagan prisoners. The Warden had the chains removed from Minota's limbs and washed to remove the bloodstains. He asked the Christians to put Minota's body on a bamboo litter and wrapped in a white cloth. Then he sent a messenger running to Minota's village some hours away to call his family to come and collect the body.

The official report would say, "Died of disease: fever and pneumonia," and the whole matter covered up — for a time. There would be no investigation and no autopsy. The word 'murder' would never be mentioned.

༄༅

Now here was Kebba, Minota's son, standing before me on the windy hillside. He has just come from burying his father. He had heard the real story of how his father suffered and was killed. And he asked me, "My father died for Jesus Christ, didn't he?"

"Yes Kebba," I replied, "Your father died for the Lord Jesus Christ. What are you going to do for Jesus?"

The young man hung his head and was quiet for a while. Then he looked up and said, "Mr McLellan, if my father died for Jesus Christ, the very least I can do is to live for Him."

In the following months, Kebba took his father's place among the believers. He carried food to the prisoners and housed and fed some of the refugees. The next year he went to Bible School to study the Bible and prepare for full-time service. Then Kebba went over the mountain ranges to the west, taking the Gospel of Christ to those still in darkness. He was used by the Lord to win many to the Saviour and he started churches in several villages.

As he remembered his father's faithful witness and sacrifice, Kebba did all he could do. Each day he would live for Jesus.

As I think of Minota again today, I have to bow my head. I remember that Jesus Christ, God's own Son, died for me. He shed His blood that I might be saved for all eternity. And I ask myself, "What is the very least I can do for Him?" With Kebba, I say that, "I must live all my life for Christ to make Him known."

What is the very least you can do for the Saviour, Jesus Christ?

5

NANA

The Invisible Man
ಹಿ❀ಜ

As the enemy came down towards him, Elisha prayed to the Lord, "Strike these people with blindness." So He struck the men with blindness, as Elisha had asked.

2 Kings 6:18

It was a time of terrible persecution in Gofa Province. It was also the time when, in answer to prayer, the Lord called Ethiopian national missionaries from Wolaitta to preach the Gospel of Christ. Nana was one of forty-two evangelists who brought their families to Gofa. Nana settled in Mallo. All the evangelists rented land, built grass thatched bamboo houses for themselves, dug up land for gardens and planted sweet potatoes, spices and a small clump of sugar cane. They sowed crops of maize, worked alongside the local people and told them about *Eyesus Kiristos* ~ Jesus Christ. They gathered the children and taught them to read and told them stories about Jesus. They boiled large pots of coffee, added salt and butter to it ~ and invited their neighbours to drink it with them and told them about Jesus. They shared their testimonies and the news that Jesus Christ delivers them from fear — fear of death, evil spirits, power of *Shaitan* ~ Satan and the spirits of their ancestors.

Several of the languages spoken in the province, such as Gofa, Zala, Uba, Mallo and Basketo were, with varying percentages of differences, dialects of their own Wolaitta, so some of the evangelists were readily able to communicate the Gospel message. Other languages, like Aari, Oyda, Galila and Dimae, were quite different, but because many of those tribal people spoke several other languages besides their own, they too could hear the Good News of salvation by faith.

Soon a few people, in a score of villages, believed the Good News and accepted Christ as their Saviour. Then they built small *selot bet* ~ prayer houses where they met together on Sundays and often during the week to learn more about the things of God. As the new believers grew in number and in their faith, changes began to happen in their lives.

༄༅

The changes also started to affect society. The witchdoctors became upset as the believers stopped taking animal sacrifices and gifts to them. The Orthodox priests were disturbed because the Christians no longer paid the 'priest's tax' to them. Government officials found that the 'Jesus People' no longer paid them bribes and would rather suffer unjustly than to do so.

A police lieutenant arrested the evangelist Atero, had his wrists chained and then his ankles clamped together in heavy iron rings so he could not walk, only hop. He then paraded Atero before the market-day crowd and proclaimed that this would happen to any who followed the 'new religion.' He told Atero, "Go back to Wolaitta where you came from and take your Jesus thing with you! We don't want your Jesus here!"

Atero hopped forward and said, "O Sir, listen. Please listen. I can go, but the Gospel will stay. By the power of God I planted Jesus in Gofa. He is planted in the hearts and souls of the Gofa people. I can go. Jesus will stay."

Orthodox priests, Government officials and witchdoctors, soon came to recognise the new 'Jesus People' as a threat to their incomes from bribery and corruption and to the control they had held over the tribal people for generations. They saw the Wolaitta evangelists and the missionaries as the cause of the changes and together they determined to stop the spread of the 'new religion' in Gofa.

Many times threats were also made against our family. One night our Amhara landowner came secretly to inform us that a mob planned to kill us. For a week he put armed guards on the road from the town to fire shots into the air to warn us if they came. If the worst came to the worst for Vida and me, he promised he would personally take our children to Addis Ababa and deliver them safely to the SIM Mission. Rumours flew around and things were very tense for some time, but we carried on our work as usual. Vida's ministry to sick people who came to the Clinic was much appreciated, no doubt contributing to the easing of tension.

Then dozens of police were sent to seize all the Wolaitta evangelists and the men who had built prayer houses on their land. Of the forty-two evangelists, forty-one were arrested at their monthly prayer and fellowship meeting, along with a dozen Gofa elders who led the work. They were all beaten and imprisoned in chains in the Bulki gaol. Throughout the province, gangs of thugs burnt down all the prayer houses. Dozens of the believers' homes were also burnt and their possessions, food supplies and animals stolen. Many believers lost their land and had to go to other areas or hide in the forest or in caves.

In one village, three church elders were shot, while some believers were beaten to death or kicked, whipped and abused, as their prayer house were burnt down. Some had bones broken and wounds left untreated. With the loss of their possessions, they suffered great hunger and misery, some times reduced to eating roots, leaves and berries they found in the forest.

For a time it looked like the priests, police and witchdoctors had won the day. Were not all the prayer houses burnt down? Were not all the Bibles destroyed? Were not all the 'Jesus People' scattered? Were not all the people now too afraid to accept the new teaching? Did we not have all the Wolaitta preachers in prison? Of course they were finished!

༄༅

Not so fast, Satan!

There is still one evangelist not accounted for! But, he is **NUMBER 1** on our **MOST WANTED LIST**! We have a price on his head! All the police, officials and some hired hunters — everyone is looking for him. Surely we will have him soon! Don't be too hasty, you evil men! Don't rejoice too soon! Satan often oversteps himself. You cannot destroy the church of the living God! Jesus Christ said that all hell would not overcome His church. Yes, you can burn some buildings, kill some people, persecute those who follow Jesus, but the suffering of the believers will purify their faith and the loss of material things will focus their hearts on their real treasure — the Saviour who loved them and died for them and who has a home reserved for them in Heaven. Compared to their material losses, the value of forgiveness of sin, freedom in Christ, peace of heart and new life would only strengthen their faith.

Nana was the one Wolaitta evangelist who was not rounded up at that time. He did not try to hide. Almost every day Nana was on the road, carrying corn and sweet potatoes to the many suffering families. He visited us regularly for prayer and to collect medicines from Vida for the sick and money to buy more food in the markets. Each week he led a group of women and children to the Bulki prison gate with food for the Christians there. These 'prisoners on remand' were not fed from the prison kitchen, even when they were held for months without being charged with any crime or brought to trial because they refused to pay bribes. Nana carried each bundle of food through the prison gate right past the guards, but they did not see him. They saw the women and children outside, but they could not see Nana.

Nana was easily identifiable as from Wolaitta, but it seemed that he was invisible or the police were blind. They simply could not see him! When he passed police and officials on the road, they ignored him! At the Bulki prison gate, other visitors waited for permission to enter, but Nana walked right past the guards with loads of food. When the guards saw the women and children outside they chased them away, but they failed to see Nana coming and going right under their noses!

Nana also delivered news and messages to the Christians from their families and brought out information, which we used to appeal on their behalf to higher authorities in Chencha. For months it seemed that the eyes of the guards and police were blind. Not once was Nana ever stopped or questioned! The Governor and all his officials could not find Nana, even when he walked in their very presence. The Police Chief, who had his hundreds of soldiers searching for Nana, could not find him either, though Nana passed them every day in the town and on country roads!

Nana was everywhere — on the mountains, in the valleys, helping people build leafy shelters in the forest, buying grain in the market places — but the enemy could not see him! And, as they tried to stamp out the fire of God sweeping across Gofa province, in doing so, they only spread further the embers of truth and freedom.

☼☙

Nana remembered how, when he was about eleven or twelve years old, the Lord strengthened and protected him. When he told his witchdoctor father that he had become a follower of Jesus Christ, Shaga hired an 'enforcer' to "beat this Jesus out of Nana." After the savage kicks, the whipping and beating he endured, Nana lay in the dust covered with cuts and bruises and unable to stand up. The neighbours saved him by screaming out the distress cry and dozens of people came running.

With cries of, "Stop! Enough! He is only a child," they stopped the beating.

Thwarted, the thug tied Nana's feet together and threw the rope over a high branch of a wild fig tree, hoisted Nana feet first into the air. Gathering sticks, leaves and dry grass, he lit a fire under the swinging boy to "burn Jesus" out of him. Once again the neighbours intervened and cut Nana down, but it was some weeks before he could walk again to the prayer house to meet with the 'Jesus People.'

Nana's father was a fourth generation soothsayer-spirit medium-witchdoctor and could not bear the thought that he might be the last. Nana's older brother Sema had told Nana of the Saviour and led him to accept Christ. Sema and their married sister had left home, so Nana was left alone with his parents. The Italian invaders had started cotton farming in the low valley and sought workers for the fields. Nobody willingly went down there because of the malaria and typhoid that was prevalent in the valley. There was also a high death rate among the workers. Nana's mother had trusted Christ too and protested strongly when Shaga gave his son to the farmers and told them to work him hard so he will forget this Jesus.

When the invaders left after the war, Nana returned home — taller, strong and healthy! Many others had died, but Nana had never been sick! It was not that he was immune from these diseases as later he suffered many times from them in the Omo River Valley. Rather, it was *"the good hand of the Lord"* on Nana's life — preparing him for future service.

Then his mother died suddenly. Nana was sad and mourned for her, but he refused to wail, dance and cut himself like the animistic people did. Shaga felt ashamed and disgraced and in a drunken rage, he picked up a spear and hurled it at Nana. Nana dodged among the cattle and escaped! A few years later Nana became the pastor of a church in Wolaitta and later, an evangelist in Mallo where he saw many come to faith in Christ. Nana's greatest joy was when his witchdoctor father, Shaga, called him home and asked him to lead him to faith in Christ! Shaga renounced Satan and became a staunch follower of the Saviour for the rest of his life.

☙☛

Now Nana, the most wanted, the hunted evangelist, led the relief effort for the suffering believers in Gofa. Like the early believers in the Acts of the Apostles 8:1-8 who, long before, suffered great persecution: loss, their first martyr, suffering; great sorrow — sadness, mourning, pain, weeping; and a great scattering — but wherever they were driven they sowed the Word of God. But then, great results — multitudes turned to Christ and great joy — at what God had done, so also the Gofa believers took the Good News of redemption, salvation by faith, with them. Despite the severity of the persecution and the suffering they endured, the Gofa Christians sowed the Gospel wherever they went. The Spirit of God gathered great numbers into the kingdom and new churches were started in scores of villages.

Praise God that today there are more than 1,000 churches in the area that used to be Gofa province! Bekele, a Gofa evangelist who had his house burnt down, had spent six months chained in prison and nearly died there because of a lack of medical attention, said to me recently, "It was tears, pain and sorrow for a time, but God worked and then there was joy and laughter." In his area, the man who led the persecution fell on hard times with sickness and disease among his herds. An old man, he apologised for what he had done. He gave the land and animals back to the Christians and also gave them another piece of land to build a large, new prayer house. His wife and most of his children and grandchildren became believers and several today are pastors and elders in the churches in the area.

The evangelists and the new believers never accused their attackers to government authorities nor sought redress for all they suffered. Instead they forgave the tormentors and prayed for them! However, during the next year, the Governor was sacked and recalled to Addis Ababa to face many accusations of corruption; the Police Chief was implicated in a failed coup d'etat and gaoled in Addis Ababa; a Bulki prison guard who murdered a Christian in cold blood was charged with an earlier murder, found guilty and executed; a false accuser who had many Christians gaoled was killed by the husband of a woman he had stolen, while many other officials and police were removed for a variety of other unrelated reasons.

༄༅

Evangelist Nana later moved to the hottest part of the Omo River Valley to work among the Bodi people where he suffered threats, abuse, isolation and much sickness for the Gospel's sake. With other evangelists he served with me in Giyu village for nine months as we sought an opening among the savage, needy Bodi warriors. The loss of evangelist Tekka who was killed by a young Bodi man, affected Nana deeply as they had worked together among the Bodi for many months. Sadly, Nana also died in the Omo River Valley, as did Jemari and Desta, who served with us among the Bodi people.

Reading this account of Nana's special ministry in that time of terrible persecution and the way God protected him, while at the same time so many others lost their freedom, possessions or even their lives, we may ask, "Why the cost?"

The Ethiopian Christians seem to understand God's 'economy' and purposes so much better than we do. Bible verses became very real and personal to them, verses like:

> *What persecutions I endured. And out of them all, the Lord delivered me. And yes, all those who would live godly in Christ Jesus shall suffer persecution.*
>
> 2 Timothy 3:11-12

and

> *They rejoiced that they were counted worthy of suffering disgrace for the Name of Jesus — and they never stopped teaching and proclaiming the Good News about Jesus*
>
> Acts 5:41-42

and

> *We must through many tribulations enter the Kingdom of God.*
>
> Acts 14:22

They claimed the promise of the Lord Jesus Christ in the *Gospel of John* as their own:

> *In Me you may have peace. In the world you will have tribulation, but be of good cheer, I have overcome the world.*
>
> John 16:33

6
LALISO
The Gold Leaves
ಶ ❋ ೞ

I, being in the way, the LORD led me.
Genesis 24:27

God did not lead them by that way, though it was near, but God led them by way of the wilderness.
Exodus 13:17-18

As many as are led by the Spirit of God, these are the sons of God.
Romans 8:14

When Vida sent a messenger with a note calling me down to the Clinic, I knew it must be important because, unless it was, she never called me off my building jobs. I found Vida examining a very sick woman. A dozen men, taking turns, had carried her for hours on a rough, bamboo stretcher up the mountain to our mission clinic. She was the wife of the evangelist Laliso who told Vida that his wife had been sick for a week with awful headaches and a high fever. She had said that her whole body was "on fire" and clutched her throbbing head. For days she had not spoken or eaten anything. The fever got worse and she was now just listless and totally unresponsive. Was it a bad case of malaria that was prevalent in the valley? Tetanus maybe? Cerebral malaria?

Vida worked really hard, using all her nursing experience, desperate to save her life. O for a doctor, a hospital, a pathology department! The nearest doctor was days away and the road impassable, closed by the flooded rivers — uncrossable. No phone or radio transmitter, no means of communication at all. We could only pray. Vida tried everything to bring her temperature down, cool sponges, different medicines. For some time nothing seemed to work. It looked like she was dying. We prayed more.

For days her life hung in the balance. Vida decided she might have typhus and treated her for that. Laliso's wife improved slightly. Vida was exhausted after days and nights of caring for her. But, the battle was won. Against all hope, Laliso's wife came around and regained consciousness and her condition slowly improved. God answered our prayers. The medicine worked. The nursing care helped and slowly, very slowly, she recovered. Laliso and his wife were so grateful. They praised God and thanked Vida over and over. And while his wife recuperated, Laliso told me his story.

৩০৫৪

Laliso had wanted to arrive in Goybi village among the Oyda people before the sun set. He did not want to be caught out in the forest where there were lots of leopards — the many traps along the trail testified to that! The evangelist started early from the valley and hoped to reach Goybi by mid-afternoon at the latest — even earlier, he hoped.

But, Laliso had not reckoned on meeting the policemen on the road! They were sitting where two trails crossed. Blocking the trail with their rifles, they demanded his name, where he came from and where he was going. Laliso had encountered their type before and was more than a bit apprehensive. There were no people around as witnesses. Laliso knew he had to be careful what he said, so he prayed silently for wisdom.

Laliso had once spent five years in gaol for walking past a flag with his hat on his head! He did not see the flagpole behind a tall tree, but that was no excuse! His protests went unheeded and he soon found himself charged with "disrespect for the country's flag" and "opposing the government." It had been a difficult time, but he had led some other prisoners to faith in Christ.

Holding his hat in his hands, he said, "Peace. Peace to you, friends. My name is Laliso. I came from down in the valley, from Sawla. I am going to find my brother." After all, he was going to find lost men who would become his brothers in Christ!

"Why? What happened to your brother? Where is he?" they asked Laliso.

"He left Father's house and went away in the darkness. He is lost and I must find him and bring him back. Father loves him and wants him to return. I think he is over the mountains." Laliso replied.

"Has your brother been gone long? How long will you look for him?" asked the police.

"Yes, he has been gone a long time. But, I will keep looking until I find him and bring him back to Father," Laliso said.

It was obvious to Laliso that the policemen only wanted 'a gift.' They waited for him to pay them a bribe to let him pass. They kept him there for hours! Laliso prayed for patience and tried not to show his frustration. It would soon be dark and he needed to go! He hoped other travellers would come along the trail, but nobody did. Probably news of the police presence had spread! Finally the police also had to leave to reach the next town, so they asked Laliso for money. Laliso could only say, "I have no money I can give you, but I wish you safety and a blessing from our Creator God." Reluctantly the police let him go and Laliso hurried on his way, hoping to make up for lost time.

ಬಂಃ

As he hastened up the trail, Laliso thanked God that He enabled him to be "*as wise as a serpent and harmless as a dove"* while he talked with the police. The sun had gone and soon it was dark in the forest. He followed a narrow path that ran alongside a small river. He longed for a drink, but there was no way down to the water. The bank was steep and Laliso could not see the water.

Laliso reminded the Lord that he had asked Him to lead him safely that day, but things had not gone at all well. Would the Lord now help him to reach a village safely — and soon! As Laliso prayed, the bank suddenly collapsed beneath his feet and he tumbled down into the river! He landed in the water with a great splash and was soaked to the skin! He suffered some scratches and bruises from the rocks as he struggled to regain his feet, but he was not really hurt at all. He thought that was some miracle and he wondered what else could go wrong! He was glad that he had his Bible and papers well wrapped up. When Laliso tried, in the darkness, to get out of the river, it proved impossible. There were only high, steep banks and he could not climb out.

Slowly working his way upstream through the water, Laliso tried to find something, an overhanging branch or some roots, anything that he could hang on to and climb out onto the bank. It seemed an hour or more before he found a track that came down the bank to the water's edge. The smell indicated it was a place where people came to draw water, wash clothes and water their animals. Laliso knew there must be houses nearby and he called out several times for help.

Soon he heard approaching voices. Several men came, one with a lighted tuft of grass. Laliso came dripping out of the water and onto solid ground. When he asked how far it was to Goybi, he was delighted to discover that he was right there!

The man holding the light said to the others, "He is a fair one and he came to us out of the water." This caused an excited babble among the group.

An older man asked, "But does he have them? Has he brought the gold leaves?"

The villagers were friendly and led Laliso to one of the houses where they sat him near a fire to dry out. Laliso wrung out as much water as he could from his outer clothes. He was glad of the warm fire. Behind a bamboo screen the women started to prepare a meal of boiled sweet potatoes and roasted corn and they soon had the coffee pot bubbling on the fire. Laliso was suddenly hungry and remembered how long it was since he had anything to eat!

More people came and soon the house was crowded. They all stared at Laliso and whispered among themselves. He had such a fair skin compared to their own shiny, black colour. Most of the Wolaitta evangelists are brown; some are much darker; and just a few, like Lemma, Dana and Laliso had the lightest skin tone. It was never an issue to them. Laliso wondered why the dark Goybi people were so excited that he was fair and had come to them out of the river? He sure hadn't intended to arrive that way!

The curious crowd parted to make way for a man who had just arrived. He was the village soothsayer, spirit medium and traditional medicine man. He also stared at Laliso for some time. Then he pressed his hands together and started to open and shut them, like opening and shutting a book. He kept repeating, "The leaves! The leaves! The gold leaves!"

Laliso didn't know what he meant, but the witchdoctor seemed so earnest. It must be very important! He prayed for guidance and wisdom. The crowd was hushed and waited expectantly. What a good opportunity to preach the Gospel! Laliso carefully unwrapped his bundle and was glad to find that his Bible and papers were still dry.

Laliso was amazed at the reaction of the people when he took out and opened his Bible. It had a black cover, but the edges of the pages were coloured gold. The people just gasped! They clapped their hands and cried out, "It is true! It is true! The gold leaves have come!"

The witchdoctor fell to his knees and reached out a hand to touch the Bible. "Yes, it is true. The truth has come at last. Now we can find the way to life."

When Laliso asked what they meant, the witchdoctor said, "A long time ago, before my father died, he told us that one day a fair man would come to us out of the water with some gold leaves. The gold leaves were the truth that would show us the way to life. We have waited for the truth for so long. Now you have come." At Goybi they had no books and so, no word for a book or pages — leaves were the nearest!

༄༅

Laliso said to me, "John's father (In Wolaitta, the polite way is to call a person by the name of their first child) John's father, it wasn't me. God did it. He had it all planned out. He had prepared the people. They were waiting for the Truth. They wanted to know the way to life. I was just the messenger. I just had to tell them. In the next year scores of people believed the Gospel of Jesus Christ. The witchdoctor renounced Satan and came to Christ. Churches were started in many villages. Dozens of the new believers were baptised. Other evangelists came to help me teach the new Christians. Praise God the work continues today and the Good News is spreading over the mountains and valleys of Gofa."

I could only nod my head in agreement with Laliso.and together we praised God for His grace and for the power of the Gospel to change lives. I also thanked the Lord for the brave and faithful evangelists from Wolaitta. They risked everything to obey the Lord and take the Good News of salvation to those waiting in spiritual darkness. Some have waited so long for Jesus, the Light of the World — much too long!

7

ONISA & GEBRE

A Rumour from the Lord

೩೦❀೦೩

We have heard a rumour from the Lord and an ambassador is sent among the heathen.

Obadiah 1

God has visited his people. And this rumour of him went forth throughout the whole region.

Luke 16:16-17

"Are you Jesus?" the young witchdoctor asked me. I was the first white man that the two visitors had ever seen. Startled at his question, I stepped back a pace. "Are you Jesus?" he asked me again.

"No, I'm not. I'm not Jesus and I am a long way from him." Obviously disappointed, the men looked at each other.

Slowly 'the penny dropped!' I said to them, "No, I'm not Jesus, but the Lord Jesus Christ does live here and I know Him. Would you like me to introduce you to Him?" They brightened up. That was just what they wanted! So, in typical Ethiopian style, I said to them, "Sit down here and we will talk about it." So they sat down and for most of the next three nights and two days we talked to them about Jesus.

೩೦೦೩

It really was the worst time for visitors to come. Vida and I had recently returned from furlough in Australia. A terrible persecution of the believers then started in Gofa Province where we worked. In a few months, every one of the twenty *selot bet* ~ prayer houses in the different villages were burnt down and 1,500 new Christians scattered when their homes were also burnt. Hundreds were arrested and many imprisoned for months without any charges being laid against them. They were beaten and whipped; many put in chains and some were killed.

Many of the Christians lost everything they owned when their animals and grain supplies were stolen, their possessions pillaged and their land confiscated. In one village three of the leaders were lined up against a tree and shot. In another a young man was beaten to death. In prison some were trampled and a man was kicked to death by a guard. Others faced starvation. Some died of diseases, exposure and mistreatment. Some Christians found refuge with relatives in other places, while others found caves or made temporary shelters in the forest. It was an awful time, especially for the families with small children. We tried to help as many as possible with food and medicine. Some friends carried food to the prisoners and scattered families.

ಐಞ

Then the rains started! Usually the 'early rains' lasted for six weeks, followed by a break of about two months before the 'heavy rains' arrived and they lasted for another three months. But, that year the rains continued right through for eight solid months. It was the wettest year we ever experienced. The 'early rains' started with electrical storms and violent winds and all the rivers quickly flooded.

One night a cyclone-like storm hit the area and blew down hundreds of houses and shops in Bulki town. The roaring of the thunder and the flashing cracks of lightning, the swirling wind and the pouring rain, which came from every direction, frightened us all. There had never been a storm like it! Vida handed me towels to try and stop the water pouring in under and down the sides of the closed doors and windows. But, it was in vain!

A tremendous clap of thunder shook the whole house and at the same time a lightning strike lit up the night sky. It hit the roof of our house and blew it apart! Roofing iron, rafters, battens — the whole lot blew off and landed hundreds of metres away. The remaining sheets of iron were peeled off one after the other by the fierce wind gusts. Some of them landed in the gully a kilometre away and some were never found!

The rain pelted down on the exposed mud ceilings and walls. And we had just finished painting it all! Now all Vida and I could do was to grab our children and stand with them in the doorways of the house. We just watched as the wet, black mud fell off the ceilings and walls — all over our beds, table and chairs. Soon we had at least ten centimetres (four inches) of water and mud right through the house! What a mess! It would be somewhat of an understatement to say that we spent an uncomfortable night! There were more to follow.

I had just built two extra rooms on the side of the house. They were each three metres (ten feet) square with a flat roof. The wet mud on the walls had just been completed and we knew we would have a long wait until it dried. Those two wet rooms survived the storm and we had to move in there while the house was repaired. The amazing thing was that despite the cold and dampness all around, none of us became sick or even caught a cold that year! We were very conscious of the Lord's protection. Because we lost some of our things and had our house damaged, the suffering Christians related to us, and we to them, as never before. It was a precious bonding that would not have been possible any other way. God never promised us exemption from trouble and problems, but the Lord did say he would be with us when we pass through them. That year the Christians proved with us that God's Word is true.

ಸಂಚ

In answer to prayer, the Lord had brought forty-two Ethiopian national missionaries from Wolaitta into Gofa.

These evangelists preached the Gospel and planted small churches. Then the great persecution commenced. The evangelists were quickly rounded up and forty-one of them were arrested and imprisoned, along with many of the evangelical Christians — the 'Jesus People' as they were called. Only one evangelist was missed in the sweep and he was being hunted everywhere. Nana lived about three days walk from us, over the mountains in Mallo. He was always away when they came to arrest him!

With his son, Nana was always out on the road, carrying food to the evangelists and believers in the prison and to the scattered Christians wherever they were in the caves and forest. The guards at the prison gates never recognised him. They never saw him! Nana was able to take medicines and messages to the prisoners and to bring messages out for the families. It was amazing how Nana survived. Often officials, police, priests and the guards passed him in the street, but didn't seem to see him at all.

Despite all the persecution and suffering, God was working and some still came seeking to hear the 'new teaching' that the authorities tried to destroy. The believers, wherever possible, still prayed in their homes, in the forest or under shady wild-fig trees. Above all they witnessed to their relatives and friends. Like the early Church in Jerusalem (Acts 8:1-8) the Church in Gofa scattered the Seed of the Gospel as they went and God touched the hearts of many people who would not have heard otherwise — people in prison, in the courts, governors, officials, the curious crowds at markets — and the Church was multiplied.

༺༻

On that worst of all days for visitors, in the rain and mud, with flattened houses, uprooted trees and bits of tin and broken timber lying all around, the two men appeared from over the western mountains. They had walked for two and a half days to get to our mission station at Minderae near Bulki town. They had heard a rumour, a story so incredible, that they just had to find out if it were true! Away over in their isolated, distant valley they heard the rumour.

For them it became a *"rumour from the Lord."*

One day in the open market place, they saw a trader selling clothes and buying coffee beans. To stir up interest and to get the people to gather around him, the trader told a story he had heard from someone else along the road. The man who related the story to him had heard it from someone else too. Others had repeated it before him. Bits were added as each one passed the story on. The men doubted if it were true. But, they would find out for themselves!

The younger man, Onisa, was a witchdoctor. He had inherited the position from his father. Some years before Onisa gave up washing himself or cutting his hair and nails, but like most of his profession, he regularly rubbed rancid butter and fresh cow manure onto his head. He wore only ragged shorts and a dirty piece of leopard skin over his shoulders. The older man Gebre was a slave. His parents had been slaves to a rich landowner, so Gebre was born a slave. Officially, slavery was forbidden in Ethiopia, so Gebre was called a 'servant.'

The rumour they heard was that a white man named Jesus lived on the mountains near Bulki and this man actually made new people. This Jesus would put his hands on the shoulders of a man or woman, boy or girl, young or old. Then He would turn them this way and that way and twist them around and when he had finished with them — behold! — they were completely new people. Indeed it was quite a rumour! So, they asked me if I were this Jesus.

൞൹

Meanwhile, over the mountains in the northerly direction, Evangelist Nana arrived home from another weeklong trip.

He had carried some food and clothes to distressed and bereaved families who had lost everything. He had comforted them and prayed for them and helped where he could to improve their shelters. Nana was so tired and after greeting his wife and family, he kneeled down and thanked God for bringing him back safely again.

He slept really well that night.

In the morning as Nana read his Bible and prayed, the Spirit of the Lord said to him, "Go and see Mr McLellan."

Nana replied, "Yes, Lord." But, he didn't go.

That night as he was again praying, the Lord impressed on him that he should go and see us at Minderae. But, he was still tired and again slept well. The next morning the Lord said, "Go and see Mr McLellan! Now!"

Nana quickly wrapped the hard bread made from the plantain trees that his wife had baked for the evangelists in Bulki prison. He made a fast pace to Bulki and then, arrived at Minderae just thirty minutes after Onisa and Gebre arrived from the other direction!

෨෬

For the next two days and most of the night, Nana and I were privileged to tell the Gospel story to Onisa and Gebre and introduce them to the Lord Jesus Christ — not a white man, but the King of Glory Who became a man to die for us. Both Onisa and Gebre believed the message and simply came in faith to Christ.

Before a little group of people they held their right hands high and renounced Satan, blood sacrifices, evil practices and all their sin. Then they raised both hands high and said, "Having renounced Satan and believing in my heart that Jesus is the Son of God Who died for me, I take Him as my Saviour with two hands. I will never deny Him." To give both hands is a sign of surrender, complete surrender.

How we rejoiced and praised God for His work of grace in their hearts! They made a quick trip down to the spring. Onisa shaved off all the mess, washed and came back looking on the outside like he had become on the inside — a new man in Christ! They had found out that the rumour they had heard was from the Lord was true. He made new people for: *if any man is in Christ, he is a new creation. Old things have passed away, behold all things are new.*

2 Corinthians 5:17

They asked for a Bible before they left. They could not read it, but they had believed it!

So they set off for home. It had taken them two and a half days to come, but it took eight days to go home because they stopped in every village, every market-place and on every crossing where the trails met, to tell the people that the rumour was true. Jesus indeed made new people and He had done it for them. They were different now. In the thrill of their life-changing conversion, they bubbled over in excitement and wanted everyone to know about the Saviour too! They became witnesses, evangelists for Christ.

Eventually they arrived back in their own valley among their own clan. What a story they had to tell! They went up and down the valley, telling everyone about Jesus Christ, the Son of God Who made new people. The whole valley was stirred as they saw the changes and the joy in the lives of Onisa and Gebre. Many people asked questions and wanted to know how they could find this peace and joy.

༄༅

But, when they talked of freedom and deliverance from sin and darkness, of Christ being stronger than Satan, all the other witchdoctors were upset! When they talked of freedom from fear and about the kingdom of God, the rich landowners were upset! This new teaching could break their control over the people who lived all their lives in fear of them. So they reacted swiftly and violently — these men had to be stopped!

The landowners, Orthodox priests and the witchdoctors had the police arrest Onisa and Gebre, the 'Jesus People' as they called them, for "disturbing the peace" and "rebellion." In the same market place where they had heard the rumour, Onisa and Gebre were staked out on the ground with their faces in the dirt. They each received 100 lashes from a bullwhip. From their shoulders down, their backs were cut to ribbons. Salt was rubbed into their wounds and they were chained, both hands and feet and then, thrown into prison. That would stop them! It was a lesson for anyone else who even thought about this 'New Way of Life.'

Onisa and Gebre lost everything. Naked, bleeding and in much pain, they were put with the convicted murderers. Those prisoners felt sorry for these men who had done nothing wrong. Onisa and Gebre were left in prison for nine months. Their homes were burnt down, their animals slaughtered and their land confiscated. Their wives were given to other men and their children were sold into slavery. The children have never been recovered. They were probably sent out of the country.

ಲ೦ಛ

After nine months in the terrible conditions of the prison, the prison guards released Onisa and Gebre as they thought they were more of a nuisance in prison than they were out of it! They had shared the Gospel of Jesus Christ with all the prison inmates and started a prayer meeting among the murderers! Many of those murderers had trusted in Christ too! When they served their long sentences, some of those murderers became leaders of churches that were started back in their villages.

With Onisa and Gebre released, several evangelists, including Nana and Mahae made trips into the area to preach the Gospel. I also made several trips over the mountains among the Aari people to tell of God's Son who changes the worst of sinners into saints!

Because of the harsh treatment he received, Gebre lost his health. He went to be with a Lord about a year after he got out of prison. However, by that time he rejoiced to see hundreds of his people baptised and following 'The Jesus Road' with him. Over the next five years, thousands of their tribe turned to Christ and 150 prayer houses were built in the villages. Praise God for His continuing work among the Aari people.

༄༅

So the years passed. Nearly thirty years later, I was again travelling with Evangelist Mahae in the Omo River Valley. Late one night we sought shelter at a small church. Nobody knew we were coming. We were surprised to find the ten main leaders of the whole Aari church meeting there for prayer and discussion about a problem in one of the churches. Then out of the dark corner came a much older Onisa. With a huge smile he wrapped his arms around me. What a reunion we had after all those years. Onisa said, "I thought you were Jesus!"

I laughed, "And you were a witchdoctor, the servant of Satan!" We laughed and cried and praised God together for His goodness and keeping power, for His good hand on our lives over all the years since our meeting at Bulki.

༄༅

Why did all this happen? It was not just by chance, just a coincidence, that Onisa and Gebre heard a rumour in the marketplace. This is the real reason, I believe, why it happened. Vida and I were on furlough (home assignment) and I travelled around speaking at many churches. I challenged people to get involved with us in the Lord's work in the Omo River Valley by praying for the tribes who, at that time, had never heard of Jesus Christ, never seen a Bible, nor met a missionary.

One night, in a small country church in the Riverina in southern New South Wales, two girls came to me after the meeting and asked if they could have one of our prayer cards. They said they would pray for us every day! They looked at the card, then at each other and then handed the card back to me. They asked if I would write on the back of the card the names of five of the unreached tribes in the province where we worked. So I wrote down the names: Basketo, Galila, Doko, Mallo and Sido. The girls were eleven and twelve year old sisters who shared a bedroom on the farm. Every night they knelt by their bed and prayed for Dick and Vida McLellan and our children by name. Then they turned the card over and prayed that God would send the missionaries with the Gospel to the five tribes.

On our next furlough, I was back in the same little town in the Riverina to speak at a missionary meeting. As I arranged the projector and the slides to be shown, the door opened and the two girls came in. They were now lovely young ladies. As they approached me, intending to ask what happened about those five tribes, I startled them by jumping around and saying, "You took my prayer card — what did you do with it?" They showed me the tattered old card that they had used over the years. Can you imagine their joy when I told them how the Lord had called many thousands of those people to Himself? I told them how the evangelists and I took the Gospel to Galila, Basketo, Doko and Mallo and now there were churches there. And I told them that Sido, the fifth name on the list was the area from which Onisa and Gebre came who had heard a *"rumour from the Lord."* That is why it happened — because two little girls prayed faithfully. "To God be the glory, great things He has done!"

8

TEKKA

Angels Unaware
ಌ❀ಌ

Do not forget to entertain strangers (being friendly, cordial, gracious, sharing), for by so doing, some people have unwittingly entertained angels.

Hebrews 13:2

BANG!
The bullet flew over the heads of the market crowd and just over our heads. It clipped something metal on a building and ricochetted off into space. The double, instantaneous sound of the shot froze everyone into statues and the shouting and the hubbub of the people in the market square suddenly stopped.

ಌಌ

It was just 'one of those days!' We should have listened to Tekka and gone the long way around. With evangelists Tekka, Nana and Ali, I was trekking from Giyu Bodi to Bulki. We stayed one night in a small *selot bet* ~ prayer house at Dimae Gero to encourage the local Christians. Tekka, Nana and I left early in the morning. We wanted to get across and out of the hot valley as quickly as possible. Ali found a trader friend of his in Gero who had a donkey and who was also going to Bulki. He was headed for the shops to buy salt, oil and soap to sell in the local market. Ali loaded our small bags of clothes on to the donkey and said that he and his friend would catch up with us later — after they "drank coffee."

With his long legs, Tekka strode ahead, effortlessly covering many kilometres of the track through the tall elephant grass. He went down the ravines and up the other side without a pause, while I tried in vain to keep up with him. With sweat pouring off me, heart pounding and gasping for breath, I found Tekka relaxing in the shade of a bush, refreshed and ready to go again! Flopping down on the ground, I suggested we must wait for Nana to catch up. He arrived twenty minutes later — when I was ready to go on! Nana believed, "slow and steady wins the race!" He walked slowly and steadily all day, never stopping except for a drink. I am sure he never understood why we rushed ahead!

At the foot of the Basketo Mountain we stopped long enough to wash in the river, eat the grain we had in our pockets and to fill up our water canteens. I hated this trail up the mountain, but it was the only road to the highlands. After prayer together and agreeing to meet at the top of the mountain, we started out. As I expected, Tekka got further and further ahead of me and Nana got further and further behind. I had to stop and rest many times on the climb, but Nana was still out of sight. Completely exhausted, I finally reached the top and staggered to a rock to sit down to stop my knees shaking! Nearby, Tekka was calmly talking to a local farmer about the Lord Jesus. After an hour 'Slow and Steady' arrived! Even Nana needed a rest.

Then Tekka said we should go even higher, along the ridge and up the mountains through Galila to Bulki. He did not want to go through Laska, the district capital of Basketo. Laska was just a few kilometres away and once we passed the town the trail went downhill all the way to the Irigini River. After that, a long gradual slope from the river up to Bulki, an easy trail, it was well used by travellers to and from Dimae and Basketo and by the coffee traders with their mules loaded with goods.

Nana and I immediately protested. "Why?" we asked. The road through Galila was much further, up and down hills, muddy and slippery. We wanted the easier path!

Tekka said, "There is always trouble in Laska. Every time I go there, there is trouble — every time! The farmer said that the Derg cadres are there. We should avoid Laska. I have friends in Galila and we can stay with them. Let us go that way." He pointed with his chin towards the Galila Mountains.

I hesitated. I did not want to meet up with the cadres either.

෩෬

The 'Derg' was the communist military junta that had taken over the Ethiopian government and murdered Emperor Haile Selassie and his ministers. The Derg drafted thousands of cadres, in groups of about twenty, to "cleanse the country of counter-revolutionaries and to indoctrinate the masses in Marxist Leninist ideology." It was a kind of Chinese Cultural Revolution. Students from the university and schools were swept along by their promises of "change, land reform, and freedom from bribery, corruption and exploitation." Hardcore communists who were well trained in Russian, Chinese, East German and Cuban methods controlled each group.

Thousands of 'advisors' from those countries flooded into Ethiopia to help the 'liberators' — the army, impose more and more restrictions on the people who had to attend compulsory training to learn the new vocabulary of 'socialism.' The cadres stirred up mob violence and killed rich landowners and businessmen, stealing their property and possessions. Town shops were looted and destroyed and market places often became tribunals called "People's Courts" where the rich, the intellectuals and anyone who opposed the cadres were beaten, imprisoned or executed. Thousands of Ethiopians went to prison for "resisting the revolution" or were killed or fled the country to escape the Derg. The reign of terror lasted for years and tore apart the very fabric of Ethiopian society.

The "exploiters and deceivers from the West" as they called the missionaries, the teachers in the Colleges and doctors and nurses in the hospitals were to be forced out. All the mission property, the houses, hospitals, clinics, leprosariums and schools were taken over. Some Christian leaders were killed and thousands imprisoned, some of them for years, because they refused to raise a clenched left fist and yell out the communist slogans. They proclaimed that Jesus Christ is Lord and they would follow Him. It was costly to do so.

৲৩৫৪

Tekka was looking to the Galila highlands. Nana wanted the shorter, easier way through Laska. The men behind with the donkey and our goods had not caught up with us and would not know that we had not gone the usual way. It was getting late. Should we wait for them? If we waited any longer we would be stuck in the forest overnight and that was not a pleasant prospect! That was when we should have prayed again for clear guidance! We didn't! It seemed best for us to go through Laska. By the time we got there, the market would most likely be over. Still reluctant and very uneasy, Tekka agreed to go with us through Laska.

Tekka did not stride out ahead in his usual fashion, but rather like the boy who "dragged himself unwillingly to school!" He was concerned and upset and said it was a mistake. We stayed close together and passed many people returning from the market. Half the crowd had dispersed when we arrived at the market place, but a few hundred were still haggling in the twilight over prices of coffee, grain and animals. Many were drinking the powerful whisky and several fights had started. It was a bad time to be there — the worst time. We circled around the edge of the market and nearly made it past.

Then a man shouted, "*Meesson* ~ Mission" and some cadres came running. Their leader was at least half drunk, obnoxious and belligerent.

He demanded we stop and men grabbed our arms. Cries of "*Ferangi!* ~ Foreigner!" "*Netch!* ~ White!" and "Mission!" were repeated by dozens of drunken louts who poured out of the drinking places. All kinds of threats were made.

It got worse, "Beat them! Kill them!" The leader stirred up the crowd and soon there was a chant of "KILL! KILL! KILL!"

When I looked at Tekka he had a look on his face that said, "I told you so. There is always trouble in Laska." The ruffians and drunken cadres roughed us up and pushed us through the crowd and stood us up against a wooden fence. The cadre leader sent for the rifles and soon he had nine cadres in a line — some of them much the worse for wear from the afternoon of heavy drinking. They formed into a firing squad as the mob shouted abuse and spat at us. Things looked bad and we all expected to meet the Lord very soon.

It all seemed unreal to me. Everything seemed to move in slow motion. I suddenly felt an incredible peace — a perfect calmness swept over me as I anticipated imminent death — an amazing joy as Heaven seemed so close. The promise of the Lord Jesus flashed into my mind:

> *In Me you may have perfect peace. In the world you have tribulation, trials, distress and frustration, but be of good cheer — for I have overcome the world.*
>
> John 16:33

The people abusing us from behind the fence and the mob in front of us were in an absolute frenzy, chanting, "KILL! KILL! KILL!"

The leader of the cadres, with clenched fist in the air, shouted, "Your God is dead! Your Jesus is dead! Long live Marxism!" As he pulled his revolver from its holster, the chanting crowd scattered to stand out of the line of fire. He directed three of the men with rifles towards Nana on my right, three to Tekka on my left, while the others aimed at me. It was surreal — it felt like it was in a dream — this can't be happening — the calm, the peace seemed to flow over me. Tekka and Nana felt the same wave of peace.

"Ready…" The rifles lifted. "Aim…"

"Lord Jesus, I am Yours."

"Fir…"

"BANG!"

The bullet that flew over the crowd and just over our heads hit a metal piece on a building behind us and went ricochetting off. Everyone froze.

Total silence!

Through the crowd came a police officer, followed by about ten soldiers. The officer, a Police Colonel, was a young man about thirty years old and he had fired the shot. He rapped out orders to his troops to seize the rifles and to send everyone away. He snatched the pistol from the cadre leader's hand, gave it to one of his men and ordered all the guns to be taken to the Police Station and locked away. He ordered the market place cleared and in anger rounded on the hapless cadres, telling them to report to him the next morning. In a few minutes everyone had gone. Only Tekka, Nana and I, standing against the fence, a few policemen and their Colonel, were left.

The Colonel looked at us and snapped, "Follow me." He strode off. We followed, with four police behind, hurrying us along. It looked like we were headed for the Police Station.

I thought, "Out of the frying pan, into the fire!"

Tekka still had that look on his face!

The Colonel suddenly turned left down a side street, then right down another, left again and then into a narrow lane between two high tin fences. A soldier guarded the entrance of the lane and another stood at the end in front of a metal gate. He opened the gate as we approached. There was another policeman inside the yard, but this was no prison. It was a nice house, the Colonel's own residence. He called us to enter and we stood perplexed against a wall while he gave orders to servants and soldiers.

ଛଓ

The room was cleared; the doors closed and he stood looking at us. Then he walked across to me. He smiled and in a quiet voice, said, "John's father. You are John's father?"

I could only gulp and say through a very dry throat, "Yes, I am John's father, but ..."

He interrupted and told us to sit down. We were glad to do so! Looking at Tekka and Nana, he said, "I know about you also. You are teaching the Bodis and that is good, very good." To me he said, "John's father, you don't know me, do you? My name is Tefera. A long time ago, when you were building the mission clinic and school at Minderae, I was a schoolboy in Bulki. Each afternoon after school we boys ran across to your compound and played with John. You told us Bible stories — stories about Jesus." Yes, I remembered the town kids coming on fine days to play with John — with his ball, if the truth were known! John had been only three or four at the time. I had told the boys about the Lord Jesus.

I told Colonel Tefera that John was now in University and he replied, "Good. Very good. Praise God."

The Colonel clapped his hands, a door opened and soon servants came in with warm water and a towel for us to wash our hands. They brought in lots of hot, spicy food, cold honey water to drink and finally the coffee. Nana was asked to give thanks. Colonel Tefera ate with us around the small table. We finished the meal; everything was cleared away; our hands were washed again and when we were alone, Colonel Tefera whispered to us, "It is late and dark outside, but it is better you go now — tonight. I will send a soldier with you to the edge of town. Go far before you stop. The cadres are evil. They are destroying our country. Don't return this way again. I will not be here to help you. The cadres have accused me to the Derg in Addis Ababa as anti-revolutionary. The Derg will soon call me there and probably they will send me north to the war front. Pray for me and go in peace. Be careful."

We prayed together and shook his hand with many thanks for his help. We slipped out the door and quietly followed the soldier to the edge of town. The moon came out as we said farewell and hurried on our way. Tekka led the way, but this time, Nana kept up with us all the way. In a couple of hours we reached the Irigini River, waded across, washed ourselves and rested on the grassy bank. We praised the Lord together for His deliverance.

In the moonlight, as we started up the long slope towards Bulki, Tekka had the last word, "As I said, there is always trouble in Laska — always!"

9

WAJA

The Prisoner of the Lord
ಬ೦✿ಌ

Do not be ashamed to testify about our Lord, or ashamed of me his prisoner. But join with me in suffering for the Gospel, by the power of God.

2 Timothy 1:8

Standing in the courtroom in Sawla, Waja held his hands high. His wrists were manacled and his ankles were chained together. "Praise God," he exclaimed, "A decoration for Jesus! This is like getting a hero's medal. I have received a decoration for Jesus!"

Turning to his accuser, Waja boldly continued, "You thought I would be ashamed to wear these chains. Not so! I am here today because I am a Christian, a follower of Jesus Christ. It is a privilege to wear these chains for my Lord. Thank you for decorating me."

ಬಌ

It was the middle of Ethiopia's 'Red Terror,' when communist cadres terrorised the land, wiped out all opposition to the Derg — the communist revolutionary party —and indoctrinated the people with Marxist-Leninist ideology. Churches were closed, Bibles confiscated and many of the church leaders imprisoned or killed. Business people and the rich lost their possessions and land. Those who resisted were killed and tens of thousands fled into surrounding countries. More than two million Ethiopians now live in other lands, mostly in America, Canada and Europe.

Those years of 'Red Terror' brought great suffering to God's people, but it also produced the 'home churches' where a few Christians would meet 'to drink coffee' together. During the time they sipped the coffee, they were able to pray and encourage each other and also witness to invited friends and neighbours. In this way the numbers of believers doubled during the seventeen years of the Derg — and then, doubled again! Most pastors in the churches were 'bi-vocational' already — farmers who augmented their small allowances and feeding their families from the things they grew — so they remained as 'farmers,' but cared for the believers as much as they could under the harsh Derg regime. Evangelists lost all their financial support, but planted crops or traded in the markets to keep going in their ministry.

Like many others, Waja was a 'bi-vocational' evangelist too. One of dozens of 'dressers' — medical workers — who were trained at the SIM Soddo Hospital. He was able to establish his own pharmacy at Sawla. With his skill and experience he won a good reputation and built a thriving business. His wisdom and integrity gave him wide acceptance in the town, while his clear Christian testimony put him into local church leadership. His powerful preaching at church services and conventions resulted in many coming to faith in Christ. Waja also sacrificially supported evangelists who went out to distant areas.

Then came the repressive Derg and like all successful entrepreneurs, Waja was suspected of being anti-revolution. To the communist authorities he was 'rich,' popular, and a Christian as well, so was dangerous and had to be eliminated.

ಬಂ

When I could not get into the prison through the front gate, I tried to reach Waja another way. I wanted to visit my friend before I had to leave the Gofa area, but the guards would not let me into the Sawla gaol. There is a small hill nearby, so I climbed it and was able to look down into the prison yard where a couple of hundred prisoners were sitting idly in the sunshine. But still, I could not see Waja.

I waited for more than an hour on the hill. I was about to leave when another group of prisoners shuffled out of their cells into the prison yard. These were the dangerous criminals — the murderers and political counter-revolutionaries. They were all chained on their wrists and ankles while armed guards watched them closely. They started picking the lice off their clothes and from each other's hair.

I recognised Waja among the murderers and saw that there were several other Christians I knew also chained with him. They had all been arrested when meeting with Waja for prayer and had been accused of "anti-revolutionary activities." That charge could bring the death penalty or long years of imprisonment.

Just then Waja looked up and spotted me on the hill. He passed the word along the line and soon all the Christians saw me on the hill. Waja stood up holding his manacled hands high. He pointed upwards and lifted his face to the sky. He was saying, "Goodbye. I will meet you at the feet of Jesus Christ."

I understood the message, so I also stood with my face to the sky and pointed with my hand to Heaven. "I don't think I will see you again down here, Waja, but I will meet you again at the Saviour's feet."

ಬಃಅ

This was not the first time Waja faced death for his faith in Christ. In the provincial Capital of Arba Minch, the Administrator, Ali Musa, was a cruel, vindictive and evil tyrant who had many Christians killed or imprisoned. Many civic leaders were also 'eliminated' and their properties 'liberated' by Ali Musa who was feared by all — "more cruel than Stalin, more communist than Lenin, more dangerous than Marx," was how he was described.

Ali Musa heard that Waja, over in Sawla, was an outspoken leader of the 'Jesus People' who needed eliminating. So he sent a truckload of soldiers from Arba Minch to kill Waja. On the way to Sawla, the truck was bogged repeatedly by heavy, unseasonable rain that delayed them for days. When the soldiers arrived at the Zenti River it was flooded and impassable. After waiting for three days in continual rain beside the raging torrent, they exhausted their food supplies, so they gave up and returned to Arba Minch to face the wrath of Ali Musa.

༄༅

The four-day journey across country to the provincial gaol in chains was a nightmare of pain for Waja, but he encouraged his fellow-Christians and witnessed along the way to the criminals, political prisoners and the accompanying guards. Still, the injustice of it all was so hard to bear. Waja wondered about Elsabet his wife and his family. How could they cope? Where would they get food? They were isolated in their house and could not go to the market.

The Marxist cadres had raided his house and pharmacy, stolen all his money, taken his papers and confiscated the medicines, even the latest, unopened shipment. Waja was not allowed to even give the medicines away to the government clinic where they could be used — they were left, the use-by dates to expire and become useless — the waste and stupidity of it all was beyond belief.

I wondered about Waja's wife and family too. A few local Christians were determined to care for them. They ignored the bans on communication and secretly delivered food to their door at night. I was able to leave some money for food to be bought and delivered. The Lord faithfully met their needs during those trying days.

༄༅༅

In the Arba Minch prison Waja was at first treated like all the other prisoners and forced to work digging trenches, carrying rocks and heavy timber poles. Then the lone, poorly trained medical attendant approached Waja. He had heard of Waja's skill and often asked his advice about diagnosis and treatments. Then he asked Waja to be his assistant. "We do not have a doctor," he said, "and there are hundreds of sick men. We do not have much medicine and I can't look after all the sick. You are better trained than I am. If you agree, it will give you the run of the place." Waja saw the hand of the Lord in this too.

Waja soon earned as much respect throughout the prison as he had outside. A month later the medical attendant was sent off for further training and was not replaced. The prison Warden appointed Waja in his place and gave him the keys to the examination room. Here Waja could meet privately with all who came to him for help. He also had access to the medical supply room. There he found a large supply of Bibles that had been ripped to pieces. They were taken from the Christians when Ali Musa ordered all churches to be closed. The pages were used as toilet paper. Waja found one Bible still complete and delightedly appropriated it as his own. He made a secure hiding place for the precious Bible.

He now had a meeting place, a Bible and a lamp for medical rounds. Waja gathered small groups of believers together for prayer. He taught them God's Word and they in turn won many fellow inmates to Christ. Soon there were Christians in every cellblock and hymns of praise could be heard throughout the long, dark nights. The months passed slowly and Waja often thought of his family. Was Elsabet all right? Were the children safe? Did they get enough to eat? He could only pray and trust God to care for them.

୨୦୧୫

One day a new group of prisoners arrived at the prison from Sawla. Waja was called to attend a man who was double chained, hands and feet, and had infected ulcers that needed treatment. Waja was surprised to find that he was the man who had falsely accused him and had insisted that he be chained. He had now fallen from favour with the Marxist regime and arrived in double chains himself. He cringed when he saw Waja.

Waja had the man's shackles removed and washed and treated his wounds. Only a few weeks passed under Waja's kindness and gentle ministry before the man broke down and asked for his forgiveness. Readily Waja forgave his tormentor. From then on he had an ally who did whatever he could to make up for his earlier cruelty. Together they sought to improve the lot of the prisoners. They started literacy classes. Then weaving and gardening projects were commenced which brought favourable comments from the authorities. Some inmates were taught to sew clothes and others to make wooden hand tools. Officials brought visitors to inspect the projects.

Waja kept up his main ministry of witnessing to the prisoners and guards while encouraging and teaching the Christians. The months dragged slowly by.

୨୦୧୫

Finally, after two and a half years, the day of release came. Waja and his companions gathered their few belongings together and said farewell to their fellow prisoners. All the prisoners assembled as the Warden read out the names of those to be released. The names of the eight Christians from Gofa who had been sentenced with Waja were read out and they were released. But, when Waja stepped forward, he was told, "Your name is not on the list. You must stay."

"But my time is complete," Waja insisted, "You can't keep me here." But they did.

The eight Gofa Christians said, "We came in together and we will all go out together" and they refused to leave the prison yard.

Waja's former accuser stirred up the assembled prisoners at the injustice of it all. First there was only a low murmur, then a rumble of voices and then a rising chorus of cries of "FREE WAJA! FREE WAJA! FREE WAJA!"

Soon over a thousand voices were shouting in unison, "FREE WAJA!" and their feet stomped the ground.

The noise increased as the prisoners made their protest. Never before had there been anything like it at the prison. The prisoners banged their chains or pieces of wood together. What a racket!

The Warden was alarmed and fearing a riot, called for more troops as the prisoners rattled the walls and banged on the gates, shouting, "FREE WAJA!" A messenger was sent to the Administrator, Ali Musa, and he tried to contact authorities in the Capital. The tide was turning and many felt the days of the Derg were limited. None wanted to make decisions or to take responsibility. At the gaol the prisoners called a strike and refused to work.

Waja was amazed at the feelings toward him. His life and witness had won many to the Saviour and the injustice of his treatment had shocked everyone. This was the last straw! "I'm a prisoner of Jesus Christ and I will wait for Him to release me in His time," Waja said.

A few hours later the order arrived, "Release Waja." The whole prison erupted in rejoicing! The prisoners and guards lined the path to the gate, clapping Waja as he departed. Behind him, weeping and carrying Waja's small bundle to the gate, was the man who had put him in prison. So Waja left prison after two and a half years. But ,he left behind his precious Bible hidden in a safe place in the prison.

"The way things are in our country these days," Waja said, "I might just need it again."

෴

When I met Waja soon after his release, I asked him, "When you were suffering in prison, what verse of Scripture did you think of most often?"

Waja smiled at me, *"Jesus said, 'I will never leave you nor forsake you.'"* Then he added, "Jesus Christ who made that promise is the same, yesterday, today and forever. He is always faithful and keeps us."

EPILOGUE

Waja moved with his family back to Soddo and established another pharmacy, which became very successful. His witness and clear testimony continued and I thank the Lord for knowing one who had such a heart for evangelism and church planting. Waja was chosen as the leader of the Wolaitta churches and served faithfully for many years. During his time as leader, many new evangelists went out to unreached areas. His story goes on.

I hope that one day Waja's biography (or autobiography) will be written to show how the grace of God proved sufficient in many difficult circumstances, in many sad experiences and disappointments in the life of this remarkable man, to show the triumph of faith and to bring praise and glory to God.

10

DESALEGN

Adopted for Life

Praise be to God who has blessed us, for He chose us in Him to be adopted as His sons through Jesus Christ.

Ephesians 1:3-5

You received the Spirit of adoption by whom we cry out, "Abba, Father."

Romans 8:15

The little boy sat alone crying on the dusty road. The few neighbours had buried the young woman, his mother. Then they collected their tools and jackets and hurried away. They didn't want to be involved any further. They had enough troubles of their own. The young woman was hardly more than a child herself. She died of fever, an infection of some unknown disease, untreated, alone. A woman passing by saw her body on the dirt floor near the open door of the shack and alerted the nearest neighbours. No one bothered about the boy. No one wanted him. He was just abandoned. The little grass shack where he lived with his mother was about to fall down anyway. The boy and his mother were outcasts. Not accepted by the locals. There was some story about an unknown father. Rape? His mother did not give the child a name. She had no reason to. Then, quite suddenly, she died — alone.

Like all of his neighbours, Takke was a hard-working farmer with a few acres of land. When an evangelist came to their area and preached the Gospel of Christ, Takke was one of the first to respond. To him, one of the amazing aspects of the Gospel was that God had *"adopted"* him into His family. The evangelist read from the Bible that God had, by *Eyesus Kiristos* ~ Jesus Christ, adopted us to Himself as sons. Then he read that we were no longer in bondage, but free because we received *"God's Spirit of adoption"* and we *"belong"* to His family. He also read that God redeemed us by the blood of Jesus to adopt us as His sons and gave us His Holy Spirit in our hearts to cry, *"Abbate ~ Father."* It was all so new, so wonderful! It gripped Takke's heart and mind. Takke rejoiced and shared this Good News with his wife and his neighbours. Some of them believed too, and they built a *selot bet* ~ prayer house on his land in the village.

The concept of adoption was quite foreign to the Wolaitta people. This animistic tribe feared *Shaitan* ~ the devil and his servants, the many witchdoctors who demanded gifts and sacrifices. Most of all, they feared the spirits of their ancestors who they believed never left the village and could bring bad luck if they were offended. When a man died, his brother was obliged to take the wife and have children with her for his brother. The children would be called by the dead man's name. Occasionally, out of necessity, a family might take a child of a relative who died into their home and raise it for the relative. But, that child always kept his father's name. It would inherit only its share of its father's possessions. Usually there wasn't much to inherit!

ଔଓ

One day Takke was riding his mule home from a distant market. He drove his two donkeys along ahead of him. As he passed through a small village, he heard about the sudden death of the unmarried young woman. Then he saw the little black boy on the road. He was naked, filthy and crying for food. He was only about a year old and very thin. No one came to answer his cries or seemed to care. Takke asked, but nobody wanted the boy. "He will soon die or the hyenas will eat him," said a man who shrugged his shoulders and turned away.

Takke sat on his mule, looking at the boy. He thought of his own family of three sons and two daughters. "If no one else wants him, I'll take him," he said. He dismounted, wrapped the boy in his shawl and climbed back on the mule. Then he hurried home. The villagers were glad to see him go. Now it would not be their responsibility to bury the child when he died.

Takke's wife was somewhat surprised when her husband arrived home from the market with a baby in his arms! But, she just took the baby and put him on her breast. When he was fed, she washed him and wrapped him in a cloth. She held him in her arms and sat on a small three-legged stool by the fire. Only then did she look at her husband for an explanation. Takke told her the sad story of finding the outcaste boy on a road weeping for his mother who had just died, no name, rejected, sure to die — nobody wanted him.

"I believe God sent you there at just the right time," his wife said, "Let him be our child. He is black, not brown like our other children, but he will be one of us. He will bring us happiness. Let us call him *Desalegn* ~ I have joy." That night the other children were told that Desalegn was their new brother. They were all to love him and care for him and teach him good things. The girls carried him around on their backs. The boys looked after him for hours.

༄༅

So it was that the little boy grew up as Takke's son. He was loved and hugged, fed and washed, clothed and disciplined. He did everything the other children did. He ran and played, jumped and climbed. Every year at Christmas time, like all the others, Desalegn received new clothes. That was always a great day!

When he was old enough Desalegn was sent to school with the other children. He was enrolled as Desalegn Takke. His brothers protected him from the few bullies who called the boy "black" or "stranger" or much worse. The oldest brother Gusho was very strong and no one dared hurt Desalegn while Gusho was around.

At home Desalegn looked after the sheep with his brothers, then, as he grew bigger, he watched the cattle and donkeys too. He learned to plough with the oxen, to sow the seed and to reap the harvest. With his brothers, he picked the coffee beans and dug up the sweet potatoes, peanuts and ginger roots. He collected wood for his mother's fire and cut grass with a sickle for the animals to munch on at night. Takke sometimes took Desalegn to the market where he soon learned to trade and barter.

৪০গ৪

While still a young teenager Desalegn accepted the Lord Jesus Christ as his Saviour. The lessons taught by his parents as the family read the Bible and prayed together every night, were well learned. The church elders who examined him for baptism said Desalegn knew all the answers about his faith and was ready to follow the Lord. With about 500 other new Christians from churches in different villages, he was baptised in a river not very far from the village. Vida and I were among the thousands of people watching from the riverbank.

Soon Desalegn was involved with other young people in the life of the church. Everyone worked together to build a new, much larger prayer house and to buy a piece of land which they called, "The Lord's Harvest." The Christians all ploughed the land together. Then they sowed corn, sweet potatoes and ginger. They used the crops to feed the poor, to support their pastor and to send evangelists out to reach distant tribes with the Gospel.

So the years passed. The girls married and left home. The older boys married, built separate houses for themselves, but stayed on their father's land. Takke treated them all alike. As the family grew, he purchased some more land that they worked together. Gusho became one of the leaders of the churches in their area. Desalegn came to our SIM Bible School at Bolosso for two years and became the pastor of a church. Desalegn and I became good friends and often shared ministry at church meetings and District Conventions. He married a lovely Christian girl and with the others, still farmed Takke's land. For a time there was a lot of persecution of Christians. Desalegn, Gusho and Takke spent months in prison. The opposition and suffering seemed only to strengthen and multiply the believers.

༄༅

Then Takke's wife died and Desalegn mourned for her, the only mother he knew. Takke was getting old too, and as his strength failed, he called the four boys together. He said, "I love you all. Keep following the Lord. Teach your children as I taught you. Desalegn, I adopted you as my son. I gave you my name and fed and clothed and educated you. You are mine. Now I want you and the other boys to equally share all of my property. Soon I am going to die. I am going to my Father Who adopted me. Promise me that you will all equally inherit my possessions." The four boys promised to do as their father asked. They placed their right hands on Takke's knees, as is their custom, and vowed to obey.

When Takke died a few weeks later, the family called all the Christians together for his funeral. Crowds of non-believers came to show their respects too. It was a huge funeral. There were several thousand people there. At the graveside, Gusho and Desalegn preached the Gospel of God's grace and several people came to repentance and faith. In hundreds of homes that night, the families sipped their coffee as usual, laced with rancid butter and salt and they ate the roasted corn. They also talked a lot about Takke and his boys. They discussed how Desalegn was adopted — a bit different, a stranger, with no claims or rights — but how he was given a new name, a new family, a new relationship, a new father, clothes, food and education. Most of all they talked about the new thing they had seen that day. It was unheard of in Wolaitta. It was new, strange, different. The adopted boy had been made an heir and equal with the sons! That was amazing! And it was all a free gift — "grace" the preacher called it — undeserved, unearned, just to be accepted! Many people would go to the prayer house in the following weeks to ask some more of the preacher. Some of them would accept Jesus Christ as Saviour and Lord too and would stay and join the believers.

ಸಂಬಂ

Desalegn, like most of the pastors in Wolaitta's rural areas, is a 'bi-vocational pastor.' He still farms the land with his brothers. And with his sons! They have bought extra land for the growing families of Takke's sons. Desalegn still preaches every Sunday, visits the sick, teaches the Word of God to young people, and seeks the lost. Often he is invited to preach in other places and he regularly uses "adoption" as the topic of his message.

When Desalegn gives his testimony, he tells of dying, unwanted, unloved, alone and of Takke saving him, making him his own son, making him a member of a new family, everything provided and even given an inheritance. He loves to read in *Galatians* 4:7: *"I was a slave of sin, of Satan, of death, but I was saved and became a son and heir. By God's grace alone, because Jesus shed His blood for us, we can all be free from Satan and eternal death. By faith we can become God's children and inherit all His riches in Christ."*

EPILOGUE

The last time I was driving through the Bolosso countryside, I met Desalegn again on the side of the road. What a reunion we had! He was on his way to visit an old believer who was sick and 'hoping to go soon!' Desalegn still farms the land and he still preaches the Gospel. He and his wife have six children — and also several orphans whom they have adopted!

"Lord, it's Mahae. What do you want me to do today?"

BUZDI
Proclaim liberty to the captives.

DAFARASHA
Out of the House of Bondage.

MAHAE, DICK AND NANA
Fellow workers for the Kingdom of God in the Omo Valley.

DANGO BAPTISING A NEW BELIEVER
You are strong and the Word of God abides in

NANA
"Has your God, whom you serve continuously, been able to deliver you from the mouths of lions?"

THE MOUNTAIN OF DARKNESS
To the land of darkness and the shadow of death.

ONISA AND GEBRE
A people who sat in darkness have seen a great light.

WAJA
You meant evil, but God meant it for good.

LALISO
And in a vision he has seen a man.

FANTA
The things which are despised, God has chosen.

The King of the Bodi Herd.

Bodi augur reads entrails.

Bodi women dancing.

Tekka's mother & brother.

MAF Cessna 180 at Giyu airstrip in Bodi.

Luchina and his protective son.

Luchina calls upon the Name.

TEKKA
Be faithful unto death and I will give you the crown of life.

JEMARI
To him who overcomes I will make a pillar in the House of My God.

Mahae leads a prayer of dedication in Gura, the village where Tekka was killed.

Bodi Warrior with 'kill scars.'

Hamer warrior with coloured mud cap and ostrich plume.

Two Hands!
With this hand I renounce Satan! With this hand I surrender to Christ Jesus! Full Surrender!

EMBRACE OF FELLOWSHIP
Received in the Fellowship of the Saints in Christ Jesus in Bodi.

TEACHING
Instruction — "Pray and Hear the Word."
Warning — "In this world you will have tribulation, but be of good cheer, I have overcome the world."

Gwobata
Who himself was waiting for the Kingdom of God.

Aldabo
If anyone is in Christ, he is a new creation.

Ekaso
If you abide in me an my words abide in you ask what you desire and it will be done for you.

Matewos
Blessed are the peacemakers.

Yohannis & Bergenae
You shall surround me with songs of deliverance.

BIRHANU AND HIS CASTAWAY DAUGHTER, TUTI
You are no longer strangers.

TASSO AND HIS FATHER, HEBANA
No one can serve two masters.

REBEKA AND HER CHILDREN
From that hour that disciple took her into his own home..

BELAYNESH AND MAHAE WITH THEIR SON, MATEWOS
Wherever you go, I will go.

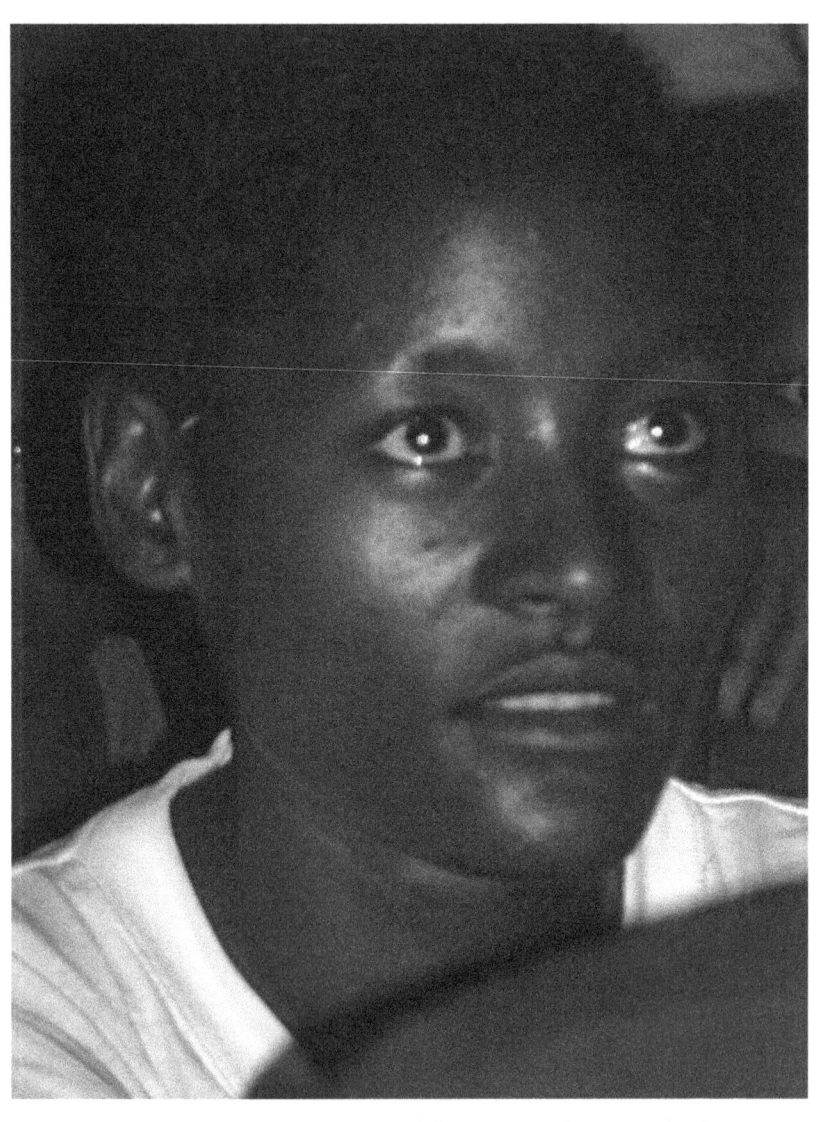

A young Ethiopian girl listens to the Word of God preached in the land of Bodi.

11

GWOBATA

The Cripple's Dream

ಬ ❀ ಡ

It will be said in that day: "Behold this is our God; we have waited for Him and He will save us. This is the Lord; we have waited for Him."

Isaiah 25:9

I have waited for your salvation, O Lord!

Genesis 49:18

Trekking with me in rough, hilly country along the Omo River Valley in southern Ethiopia were evangelists Desta, Nana and Matusel. It was an isolated place, a small valley surrounded by mountains with lots of trees, almost a forest. None of us had been in the area before, but after much prayer, we decided it was the right time to take the Gospel there. Few of the people of the first village had seen a white man before, but they cheerfully welcomed us and cleared out a small hut for us to stay in. The women roasted some cobs of corn and gave us their special coffee made from the leaves of the coffee trees and spiced with butter, salt and red peppers. We spent the evening hours sharing the Gospel with the villagers who gathered around the house and listened carefully. They asked us to stay with them and tell them more! The next day we went on to the next village, but promised we would return that night. We walked, one behind the other, along a narrow track that they said led to the next village.

"Do you have the Word of Life? Do you have the Word of Life?"

Ahead of us, sitting on the side of the trail, a man shouted out the question, "Do you have the Word of Life?"

I waved my Amharic Bible in the air and yelled back to him, "Yes, we have the Word of Life." About 200 metres ahead, the man became very excited and signalled for us to come to him.

As we hurried towards him, the man said over and over, "You have the Word of Life! You have the Word of Life!"

༄༅

In that part of Ethiopia, coffee trees grow wild in the forest. For many years the people of the area did not know the value of coffee beans. Their witchdoctors forbade the people from picking the beans so all the beans just fell off the trees and rotted on the ground. The people boiled the leaves of the coffee trees and drank that with butter and spices.

Then one day everything changed. A coffee trader from northern Ethiopia discovered the valley with excellent coffee growing in the forest. He came with his team of mules and gave gifts for the local people to bring the coffee beans to him. He gave them sacks to collect the beans and in exchange gave out some clothes, salt, sugar or lots of 'pretty beads.' The trader spread the beans out on the ground to dry in the sun. When they had dried, he loaded the sacks onto his mules and went away to make an amazing profit. Each year he came with more and more mules and stayed for two or three months in the area collecting the coffee beans, and he also learned the local language, one of few outsiders to do so.

One time, weeks after the trader had gone on his way, a young man asked his father how the trader became rich, so that every year when he came, he had more mules, more servants, more gold rings on his hands and such fine clothes. The young man, Kebede, wanted to follow the trader and get some riches for himself. His father told him not to go, but Kebede was quite determined. His father said, "Don't go. My father never left this valley, nor his father either, and I have never gone. My son, do not leave us. Think of your wife and family." Kebede had a two-year-old daughter and his wife was pregnant again. Kebede started out anyway. His father followed behind Kebede to the top of the hill, pleading with his son not to go, but Kebede kept walking. His father shouted after him, "If you go, you will never return."

ೞಞ

Kebede walked for several days along the valley. By keeping near the foothills, he avoided the Bodi and Mursi people whom he feared. He passed through several villages of Aari people. They were friendly enough, but he could not understand their language. He made signs for "food," "drink" and "sleep" and he got by for a while. But, when he became sick and weak, getting worse by the day, he could not make people understand about the pain in his stomach. He needed help — and quickly — but nobody spoke his language! He staggered on trying to reach a town, but he was overwhelmed by the pain and collapsed on the road.

Fortunately a kind man came by with a donkey. He picked Kebede up, put him on the animal and took him up the mountain to the SIM Mission Clinic at Bako where he had been helped himself. The nurse at the clinic did not know what was wrong with the man to whom she could not communicate. She cared for Kebede as best she could and treated him with several antibiotics. But, Kebede was only getting worse, so he was sent to the SIM Mission Hospital, far away at Soddo.

Kebede had to be carried on a litter over the mountains to the beginning of the road. There he was put on the back of a merchant's truck and taken for several days to Soddo. It was a frightening experience for Kebede who had never seen a truck before and could not communicate with anyone!

At the hospital Doctor Nathan Barlow confirmed the nurses' diagnosis. He didn't know what was wrong with him either! He prayed a lot and tried to explain that he would have to operate to find out what was wrong. Kebede liked the kind people at the hospital, but just looked blankly at Nathan Barlow. So Doctor Barlow operated on Kebede and as he expected, he found a cancerous growth that had spread to vital organs in Kebede's body. The doctor did what he could, removed some of the cancer, sutured Kebede up again and gave him relief from the pain. They cared for him in a bed in the Men's Ward. But, the doctor could not tell him that he was going to die. Worse than that, he wasn't able to tell him about the Saviour, Jesus Christ. Every day a Wolaitta evangelist came and preached the Gospel in the Men's Ward, but Kebede could not understand. When the evangelist showed Bible pictures, Kebede, who had never seen a picture before, could not make out what they were. Slowly Kebede got weaker. He was washed, given food and cared for, but he was going to die.

※※※

Again it became the time of the year when coffee beans were to be collected. From the north came the coffee trader with his scores of mules and all his workers. He passed within twenty kilometres of the Soddo hospital every year, but had never been there. He had no reason to do so. But, that year — and only that year — as he journeyed, he got a toothache. It became infected and his whole face became swollen, his ear, jaw and face ached and soon the merchant was in agony. In the distance he could see the shiny metal roofs of the mission station and someone told him to go there, as foreigners were there who could help him.

Doctor Barlow examined the trader, told him he would lance and drain the infection, remove the tooth, put in a couple of sutures, give him a series of penicillin injections and he would need to stay in the hospital for several days. The trader was just so grateful to get relief and after the treatment, he was put in a bed in the men's ward. So it happened that the man who had come hundreds of kilometres from the north was put in the bed next to a man who had come hundreds of kilometres from the south. What a coincidence! The only man outside that isolated valley who knew Kebede's language, landed up in the bed next to him!

༄༅

Meanwhile, over in Los Angeles in America, Joy Ridderhof was having her daily devotional time. As she prayed, Joy was impressed that God wanted her to go to Ethiopia. She was overjoyed and was soon ready to go! She had always wanted to go to Ethiopia. In fact Joy had trained to go as a missionary to Ethiopia many years before, but had never made it! The Italian invasion in 1935 intervened, then the Second World War. Joy went to Honduras instead and served there for five years before she was invalided home with severe malaria. She was unable to return to the field, but the Lord gave her a vision of tribal people who could not read the Bible. Joy started Gospel Recordings, a Mission that has recorded Gospel messages in nearly 6,000 languages around the world and supplied millions of records and cassettes to missionaries and evangelists.

With two companions, Ann Sherwood and Sanna Barlow, Joy arrived in Ethiopia and in very short time, was granted an audience with the Emperor, His Imperial Majesty Haile Selassie. He gave Joy permission to record the Gospel in the languages of Ethiopia. This was started with the help of many missionaries. So Joy and her friends went to Soddo Hospital where they were able to make recordings in several languages.

Another coincidence — Joy found Kebede and the coffee trader in the Men's Ward. The doctor, nurses and the evangelist had used the coffee trader to translate for them as they told Kebede how he could be saved from his sin. They all rejoiced when Kebede accepted Christ as his Saviour. Joy used the SIM missionaries, the evangelist and the coffee trader as her language helpers as sentence-by-sentence, phrase-by-phrase and word-by-word, she recorded several short Bible stories in Kebede's language. Joy soon went on her way rejoicing.

The coffee trader, healed with his face back to normal, went on his way to make his fortune. And the rogue, when he arrived down in that distant valley, never told anyone that he had met Kebede in the hospital. It took another ten years before news of his death reached his waiting family. Yes, Kebede died at Soddo and was buried in the little graveyard near the hospital. As his father had predicted, Kebede never returned to his family.

༄༅

And the years rolled by! The recorded messages went to America where they were put on to 78 rpm records. The records were sent back to Soddo hospital, then on to us at Bako. When we played them in the Clinic, the marketplace and in the villages, nobody understood them, so we put the records aside. When we moved to Bulki and played the records again, someone said they thought the language was a dialect of the Dimae tribe, over the mountains to the west. The records were put away again — in a box under the bed — and silverfish ate the labels. We left the records behind when we moved on again to start another mission station — and the years rolled by! Eventually other missionaries recorded those records onto a cassette. Because they could not read the labels, they wrote on the cassette, **"Language Unknown."** When the missionaries were forced out of Bulki by the communists they had to leave some things behind. When I came through Bulki on my way to the Bodi tribe, I found the cassette and took it with me. I thought I might find the people who spoke the language.

༄༅

"Do you really have the Word of Life?" the man shouted again. As we came nearer, we saw that he was an old man with both of his legs crippled. He could not stand. He'd had an accident many years before that broke his legs. Without proper treatment, he was left a cripple. He was only able to drag himself along by his hands, sliding on his bottom. He was sitting on the bank above the washed out trail. Here he was — a congregation of only one — and there were four of us missionary preachers, so he 'got the treatment!' I mean that he had a clear presentation of the Good News of Jesus Christ given to him! Over the next two hours we took it in turns to tell him the "old, old story" of God's love and grace.

Gwobata (for that was his name) had never seen a Bible or heard a missionary before, but he sat there enthralled — just like a sponge drinking up water! It was exciting for us just to watch him! The more we told him about Jesus, the more questions he had! But, we had to go on our way, so we left one of the evangelists, Desta, with Gwobata, to explain more of the Way of Life. We left him with a small cassette player and two cassettes, one of which was the trade language, but Gwobata did not know that language. The other cassette was the one marked, **"Language Unknown."**

It was late in the afternoon when we returned. A large group of people had gathered. Desta was having a rest under a shady bush, but Gwobata was still listening to the cassette player. The batteries were almost flat, but he had it pressed to his ear. Some of Gwobata's family and neighbours had joined him and Desta at the roadside.

Desta said that Gwobata was ready to believe in Jesus Christ as his Saviour. He could not stand up, but he held his right hand high and renounced Satan, spirit worship and blood sacrifices. Then with both hands held high, Gwobata accepted Christ "with two hands," as they say, meaning complete surrender, with no reserve. We rejoiced and prayed with him. Then Gwobata wanted his family and friends to receive Christ too! He told us that the voice on the tape was that of his own son Kebede who had left long ago and never returned. That day we met Kebede's wife, who had remarried, and his two daughters, now grown up and married too. We were privileged to lead them to Christ also. What a wonderful day it was!

I asked Gwobata why he had called out when he saw us coming. He told us that one night, in his little grass hut up the hill, he had a dream. In the dream there was a man running down the trail, through the darkness, shouting, "The Word of Life is coming! The Word of Life is coming! Believe the Word of Life and you will live forever!" It was strange dream. In that area, because of the wild animals, huge pythons and poisonous snakes, no one travels at night.

However, the dream was so vivid that in the morning Gwobata dragged himself down to the trail. He waited for someone to come along and he asked if they had the Word of Life. They had no idea what he was talking about and passed by. All day Gwobata waited. He asked every traveller, but nobody could help him. In the evening his family took his arms and dragged him back up the hill to his house. But, first thing next morning he slid down the hill again and asked everyone the same question. And the next day, and the next, and the next! I asked Gwobata how long he had waited by the trail for the Word of Life. He said, "Twenty years."

No wonder he was excited when we told him that we had what he had waited for — the Word of Life! I cried that day that a man wanted to hear the Word of Life and had to wait for twenty years to do so! In my heart today I still cry that there are so many others waiting for the same wonderful message of redemption, forgiveness and eternal life.

EPILOGUE

A couple of months after we met Gwobata, the communist authorities forced all of us missionaries, foreign and Ethiopian nationals, out of the Omo River Valley. It was fifteen years later that I was able to return to the Omo area and I received a letter from Evangelist Girima. He told me how God had led him into that area where he had found a small group of Christians. He had spent six months teaching them the Word of God and preparing them for baptism. Girima asked if I could come and speak to the candidates. I was thrilled to hear what the Lord had done in that area. Evangelist Mahae came with me and we drove into Bodi country again. We stayed overnight at the police post at Hanna, left the vehicle there and the next day walked up the mountain and back into Gwobata's valley. Because we were told it would take "six or eight hours," we left early — at first light. It was a very hot day and the mountain seemed much steeper than it had been fifteen years before! It took us eleven hours to get there after many stops to rest on the way, but what a privilege it was to share the Word of Life with the people again! I was sad to learn that Gwobata had died some years before. He was faithful to the Lord to the end of his life and the animistic people said they gave him a 'Christian funeral.' The next day, the first man baptised was Gwobata's brother. Then twenty-five more believers followed him into the water. Since then many more people have believed to followed the Lord in baptism and there are *selot bet* ~ prayer houses established in several villages. Praise God for His grace and guidance! I believe the many 'coincidences' of this story are really Divine interventions so an old crippled man, and his people, could hear the Word of Life and come to the Lord Jesus Christ and be saved. I hope you think so too!

12

TEKKA

A Martyr for Christ
ಬಿ✿ಲ್ನ

No one who puts his hand to the plough and looks back is fit for service in the Kingdom of God.

Luke 9:62

Nearly thirty years ago, in March 1977, I wrote the following account:

> Evangelist Tekka Mihael became the first martyr for Christ in taking the Gospel to the Bodi people when he lost his life recently near Gura. He disappeared among these cruel, darkened people in December while on a preaching tour of Bodi villages. He had delayed the trip for a week waiting for me. We had planned to go together, but a severe bout of cerebral malaria and dysentery kept me away. Other evangelists offered to take my place, but Tekka felt he should go alone.
>
> Tekka left Giyu before Christmas with a burning desire to bring Christ to the Bodi warriors in villages and cattle camps along the Omo River. He promised to be back in time to see the Missionary Aviation Fellowship aeroplane, a Cessna 180, land for the first time on the airstrip at Giyu that he had helped prepare. He wanted to spend Ethiopian Christmas (January 7th)

with Nana, Kassa and me at Giyu to show the local Bodis the meaning of Christmas.

Tekka travelled with few possessions — his Bible, a booklet with pictures of New Life that he used to explain the way of salvation, a water canteen and a packet of razor blades to trade for food. He wore a light cloth over his shirt and shorts.

As days went by and became weeks, we asked people to pray, listed him as missing and began a search. Other evangelists went in teams to look for him while neighbouring 'friendly' Bodi men crossed the Omo River and soon reported that Tekka had not gone that way. Weeks of enquiries revealed that Tekka spent a night among the cattle herders at Gura, drank some milk with them in the morning and left for another village. He went along a trail through the bush, but he never arrived. While we were rejoicing in God's gift at Christmas, Tekka was no doubt rejoicing in the very presence of the Lord Jesus Himself — the Saviour he loved and served so fervently.

...

Tekka was born to a poor peasant couple about forty years before in a small Dimae village. Hot, malarial valleys surround Dimae, a group of rugged mountains. Thick forests abound and cool streams tumble down the rocks and sweep through Bodi country to join the Omo River. Mount Smith, its 9,800 foot peak often shrouded in cloud, overlooks the small Dimae area. At one time the Dimae people numbered 25,000, but tribal wars and disease have reduced their numbers to about 2,000 today. Ruins of round, stone houses, stone fences and wonderful terracing abound in the forest, swallowed up by the vines and trees. Men dig iron ore from the ground and smelt it in homemade clay furnaces, which are heated furiously by half a dozen men sweating on bellows made from goatskins. Tools for ploughs, axes and hoes are made in this way, as are knives, spears and large machetes. Like his parents, Tekka grew up in the fear of darkness, demons and witchdoctors. The Dimae people are animists who fear the spirits of their ancestors and make sacrifices through the witchdoctors to evil spirits and to Satan.

Tekka developed quickly into a big, strong lad. He learned to dig the fields, plough with oxen and to guard the cattle herds of the cruel landlord and his spiteful wife who kept the people as virtual slaves on their own and on free land. The landlord liked to humiliate Tekka by giving him heavy loads to carry and calling him, "Donkey." Beatings, whippings, kicks and abuse became the norm, but long days in the heat of the valley hardened his body. Tekka carried loads hundreds of kilometres over rough trails for the landlord as he collected taxes, gifts and bribes. During all this travelling, Tekka picked up five languages and learned his way around the Omo River Valley.

Tekka's older brother had fled from Dimae to escape the slavery about fifteen years ago and never returned. His mother kept Tekka at home though she grieved for the hardness of his life. Tekka married Gilande, a small Dimae girl and they had a daughter, but his wife died of fever two years later. Tekka then married the wife of his brother who had died, but she also died — of typhoid fever. Several other women came and went, but Tekka found little rest or happiness. When his daughter died of malaria in that isolated area, Tekka was crushed beyond measure. A wild restlessness possessed him.

The nearby Bodi tribe again started to make raids on Dimae villages. People were afraid, but Tekka hoped for a chance to fight. The Dimae people were decimated. They found the Bodi warriors were experts at dawn raids, killing, looting and driving off the animals. Even the landlord started losing his cattle herds. Then anthrax broke out among the remaining cattle and Tekka lost the few he had. Family, possessions and even hope had all vanished.

...

From over the mountains, rumours of a 'new teaching' drifted through the weekly markets. They told of 'a new life,' of a Deliverer stronger than Satan and death, of foreigners with a new religion, of a Book of Life and of evangelists that officials opposed, beat and imprisoned. Warnings were given not to listen to this Good News.

Tekka wondered if it could be true — freedom, new life, peace! He hoped that it was true.

The hard life under the landlord continued year by year. The witchdoctors were just as demanding and Tekka often talked with his friends and they wondered if there was a better life. They heard rumours that the 'new teaching' had come into the neighbouring tribes, Mallo and Galila. Maybe it was true! Some people evidently thought so! Tekka heard that in Gofa the 'Jesus People' were in prison and their 'prayer houses' — whatever they were — were burnt down. Now there were preachers in Basketo and Aari — the nearest tribes to the Dimae. Maybe they would come to Dimae too!

In the mid 1960's a new scourge swept along the Omo River Valley — Yellow Fever! Unknown in this area, the disease soon passed through a dozen different tribes and thousands died. Everywhere relatives, friends and neighbours died. Whole villages were wiped out! Tekka was sick for weeks, but he recovered. However many of his people died and Tekka was in despair! Everything was gone. In dark hopelessness, Tekka cried out for help.

...

In 1970 Tekka heard startling news! The chief Dimae witchdoctor had fled! It was said that Dano the witchdoctor had gone to Mallo and had become a 'Jesus man.' He had renounced Satan and was a new person — changed, clean, happy. Some months later Dano returned with a preacher, Daniel Choramo, Mahae's brother. The two of them went everywhere telling people about Jesus Christ, the only one who could save from sin and give peace of heart.

Tekka was their first convert! Sick of sin and slavery to Satan and to men, he found new life in Christ. He came wholeheartedly to the Lord — never any half measures with Tekka! Soon he learned to read the Scriptures and was baptised. Later he went to Bible School in Bulki for a year. He left the landlord who later was dispossessed of all his property and was imprisoned in the change coming to the land. By leaving, Tekka lost his land, home and gardens, but he managed to sell his few animals and hide the money with his mother. She still has it.

...

Tekka was 'sold out' for Christ right from the start. It was soon evident that God had further plans for this lonely man. He lost interest in possessions, caring little about food or clothes or where he slept. He learned God's Word, spent much time praying and was soon preaching New Life in Christ in the villages throughout Dimae, often accompanied by Dano or one of the growing band of believers. Tekka's father had died about twenty years ago, but Tekka won his mother, younger brother and sister to Christ about three years ago.

Every day Tekka learned more and grew in the things of Christ. Somewhat of a 'loner,' he had little patience for anything less than wholeheartedness in devotion and obedience to the Lord. A rugged individualist, he had a heavy burden for those who had not heard the Good News of salvation. He possessed a driving urge to go on and on into unreached villages with the Gospel.

Then came the savage Bodi raids of 1975 across the Omo River in Boroda Konta. Hundreds of Christians lost their lives among nearly 3,000 killed that year. The fifteen 'prayer houses' were destroyed and whole villages left deserted as thousands fled to other areas. Vida and I had had an outreach in that area with the Wolaitta evangelists. As news of the massacre spread, people around the world started focussing prayer on the Bodi tribe.

. . .

When the first trek was made in August 1975 across 'no-man's-land' to five Bodi villages, Tekka was there with Nana, Kassa and me. He knew most of the trails and the Bodi language and he was thrilled to make this contact and to witness for the Saviour. When we returned from that ten-day visit, Tekka came to tell me that God had called him to take the Gospel to the Bodis. He had given himself fully to the Lord for the task.

Tekka and Nana returned to Bonke village that we had visited. For months they lived there in constant danger of being murdered at any time by the cruel young men. By Bodi custom, young men have to kill a man of another tribe to be eligible to marry. For some time they were kept virtual prisoners in the village. Nana had to stay when Tekka went back to Dimae or to Bulki for supplies.

After six months they were able to leave — just before the Bodi warriors again went on their raids. In 1976 about 500 people were killed in Mallo and Dimae and hundreds of cattle stolen. People again scattered in every direction.

In August 1976 Tekka, Nana, Kassa and Jemari came with me to the Bodi village of Giyu. This was the centre of the Shirm clan and had a small creek that only dried up in the hottest, driest of years. From there we reached out to the Bodi villages around. Tekka and I walked hundreds of kilometres together to tell the story of Jesus over and over again. Often we slept under the stars or crawled into a Bodi hut. I found the burning sun, the incessant heat, and the rough tracks through the thorn bushes, the bush ticks, the flies and the plagues of malarial mosquitoes really trying. Tekka hardly seemed to notice them, but was very patient and tolerant when I complained or wanted to rest.

...

Tekka's prayers were original and sometimes unusual, but none could doubt his sincerity and devotion to Christ. He always started, "O Lord Jesus, here I am. I'm Tekka. I am praying." He could never be a diplomat. He was guileless and transparent and frequently quite blunt in things he said. He was not clever, but so faithful; not a scholar, but a keen learner and so trusting — trusting and trustworthy. Tekka was fearless among men and women who are murderers. I clearly remember the last prayer I heard Tekka pray, "Lord Jesus, when will I see you? I want to stand before you. You are my life, my only joy."

Once, as we trekked together from Bodi to Dimae, we paused for breath at the top of a hill. We could see many kilometres of the Omo River Valley with the tall 'elephant grass' waving back and forth in the breeze. Tekka pointed with his chin to another trail on the next hill. He said, "That is where God stopped me being afraid of the Bodis."

I replied, "Please, tell me how it happened."

Tekka said, "The Bodis were raiding everywhere, ravaging all the country around Mallo, Basketo, Dimae and Kafa. My friend Nana was held hostage in that Bodi village, but they let me go to Bulki for supplies of food and medicine. As I went, I passed three Bodi men with guns. They knew me and let me pass them. Soon I heard crying and shouting — a great noise. On the road ahead nine Bodis with guns and clubs were beating a Dimae man to death. He was a Christian friend of mine, but I could do nothing. His bones were broken and there was blood everywhere. They had tortured him and killed him before I arrived."

Tekka wept as he relived the pain of that scene. "A tremendous fear seized me and I started shaking all over. 'Today I die,' I thought and I plunged off the trail into the grass. I was terrified and couldn't stop shaking. Falling on my hands and knees, I cried out to God in prayer. My mouth opened and shut, but my voice was lost to me. I could not breathe and my hands fled here and there. So I prayed in my heart, 'My God, Lord Jesus Christ, take this fear away and still my body. I will be faithful to You and preach today and every day. If they kill me, I will go and see You face to face. I have nothing to lose.'"

"Then the Lord took away all my fear — all of it — and peace flowed over me like water. With new strength I rose up and went to the place of death. The nine men had guns, knives and clubs in their hands, but when they saw me, all those Bodi warriors turned away their faces. They were ashamed.

I told them of the wonderful Lord Jesus Christ and about the 'new life way'. Then I picked up the body of my friend and I carried him to his house and I buried him there. The Bodis wondered why I was not afraid of them, but I died to this world that day. I have no home, no land, no family, no possessions. I belong only to Jesus and in future will only serve Him to tell the Bodis His way."

I see Tekka now — what a great walker he was — striding through the tall grass with a load on his head, setting a pace that left us all gasping. I remember him racing the young Bodi warriors down the newly completed airstrip at Giyu and leap-frogging high over one's head. How he enjoyed life! I see Tekka squatting on the ground, slowly explaining the flipchart, "New Life in Christ" or crawling into a Bodi hut. He truly *"sat where they sat"* because like the prophet Ezekiel, *"the hand of the Lord was strong upon him."* His vision was for unreached tribes; lost souls in the spiritual darkness he, himself, had so recently escaped. Tekka would go anywhere to tell people about Jesus Christ and longed to go across the Omo River to the other savage clans of Bodis there. That is where he was headed when he left Gura.

...

How did Tekka die? We discovered that while he drank milk that morning (most of the cows at Gura were stolen from Boroda or Mallo) a young man ambushed him on the trail leading through the bush. Tekka was shot, stripped of his clothes, his body mutilated. Tekka's killer ate part of his heart, drank some of his blood, decorated himself with Tekka's clothes and blood and earned himself a great reputation as a killer of men. We are not sure of the details of his death — they are not important — we hope he didn't suffer. We do know for sure that Tekka died as he wanted to — taking the Gospel of Jesus Christ to souls in spiritual darkness and sin.

I am writing this sitting on the dirt floor of my grass hut in Giyu Bodi. Tomorrow I must go to Dimae to tell Tekka's mother, sister and brother that he is with the Lord. It is not going to be an easy task. I thank God for my brother Tekka, a simple Christian, so brave, so vital — *"of whom the world was not worthy."* I'm sure Tekka had no regrets. His favourite text was, *"to be with Christ which is far better."*

...

Let us commit ourselves anew to the Lord Jesus Christ to speed the Gospel to these needy Bodis. Let us claim Gura and its people for Christ. May Tekka's blood be a sign to these lost souls and become indeed 'the seed of the church.' Let us covenant with God to pay whatever is necessary to make it so.

Dick McLellan
Giyu, Bodi, 1977

You who call on the LORD, give yourself no rest and give Him no rest...
Isaiah 62:6-7

...

EPILOGUE

Now it is June 2006.

Some things are much different in Bodi today. A few months after Tekka was killed, the communist government drove out the missionaries from the Omo River Valley. Then the Ethiopian evangelists had to leave and there was no Gospel witness in the Bodi area for about twelve years, though Jemari and Nanna contacted a few Bodis in the Dimae market.

Besides the continual malaria, dysentery and tuberculosis, epidemics of cholera, meningitis and yellow fever swept through the valley and a disease wiped out most of the cattle. This led to more raids by the Bodi warriors on surrounding tribes to replenish their herds. Army troops were then sent in to stop the raiding. They killed many of the Bodi warriors and gaoled the chiefs of the Shirm and Gura clans.

The police post at Hanna was strengthened to a large station, a weekly market was started, some wells were dug, a medical clinic commenced, an elementary school was opened and a boy from each Bodi village or family was compelled to attend. Slowly improvements were made and a gravel road was built two years ago, so supplies can come in by truck and Hanna has become a small town.

☼☼

With the end of the communist government in 1991, evangelists were again able to come in from Gofa, Mallo, Basketo and Dimae. They settled in Hanna and Giyu. They found many people were gone and they now reach a new generation. There is no more talk of "eating the old men to get their strength" or of raiding to steal cattle. Parts of the valley have been taken over for settlements of people from distant tribes and corn, millet and sweet potatoes have been sown. Even some of the Bodis are learning to farm the land.

Armed police hunt down the murderers and courts in Hanna deal out justice.

Evangelists Tekka, Desta, Nana and Jemari have all gone to be with the Lord and only Kassa and I remain of the original group at Giyu. I have been back there six times to encourage the evangelists and to reach out to more villages along the Omo River. Prayer houses have been built in Giyu and Hanna and in several other places. A young people's group in Hanna town has seen many teenagers believe in Christ and be discipled in God's Word. The young people are from all the clans, but most are from the Gura clan.

ಬಿಂಬ

In January 2005 a long-forgotten prayer of mine was answered. Our son John, Mahae and I found the village where Tekka was killed. We prayed there with the evangelist who took us into the new prayer house that is built on the spot where Tekka was shot — he died instantly — thankfully he never suffered. We saw the space where the Bodi women all danced and sang, "We have eaten other men, but Tekka is sweeter than them all."

The first Bodi convert from that village in Gura has gone to Bible School in Jinka. We visited him there. What a sight it was! Mabeye sat in the midst of students from five different tribes that used to be bitter enemies who would kill each other on sight — now all brothers in Christ. They learn God's Word together, eat together and play sport together, live in the same dormitory — peace in the Omo River Valley — amazing! Only the Lord Jesus Christ can change people like that! Tekka did not die in vain!

> *We are treated as unknown and ignored by the world, and yet we are well-known and recognised by God and His people; as dying, and yet here we are alive; as chastened by suffering and yet not killed; as grieved and mourning, yet we are always*

rejoicing; as poor ourselves, yet bestowing riches on many; as having nothing, and yet in reality possessing all things.

2 Corinthians 6:9-10 (AMP)

ଚ୍ଚ ❋ ଓଓ

13

JEMARI

Culture Shock and Courage

ಲ ❀ ಛ

Endure hardship as a good soldier of Jesus Christ.
2 Timothy 2:3

Endure afflictions, do the work of an evangelist, fulfil your ministry.
2 Timothy 4:5

Jemari was the only Ethiopian I knew to experience genuine 'culture shock!' Jemari was born and had grown up in a culture of fear. His father and countless generations before him were taught to fear. They were afraid of Satan, the spirits of their ancestors, of evil spirits, of death and especially afraid of the witchdoctors. They were powerful, dangerous and always demanded 'gifts' of animals to make blood sacrifices to the powers of darkness.

Then one day the evangelist Nana came to the area where Jemari lived in Mallo. Nana started preaching something new — the Gospel of Jesus Christ. Jemari and other young men listened eagerly to the new teaching and spread the news to the villages around — "*Eyesus Kiristos* ~ Jesus Christ is stronger than *Shaitan* ~ Satan and can free us from fear and give us new life." Some older men responded to the Gospel message. A couple of families believed. Then a witchdoctor was converted. The powerful Chief of Mallo came to Christ. Persecution started from Orthodox authorities with much suffering and some *selot bet* ~ prayer houses were burnt down, but the number of believers increased. Several times Nana and Jemari, along with other young Christians, were imprisoned, often for months at a time.

Then Jemari went to the Bible School at Bulki to study the Word of God and soon started to preach the Gospel also. In 1975, Nana joined me for the trip to make the first contact with the unreached Bodi people. We were also to survey the needs of people living along the great Omo River. Jemari and a young Wolaitta evangelist, Munae, carried on the work in Mallo. Nana had spent much time in Mallo to mentor and train several young men, including Jemari and Munae, to become true *"soldiers of Jesus Christ"* for the spread of the Gospel.

A year later, Nana left his home and family in Mallo and went to live and witness among the Bodi people. He also left behind a growing church. To pastor the believers, Nana chose Jemari. Although young and quite timid, Jemari had a strong faith and a deep love for the Lord Jesus Christ. Tested by suffering himself, he had a powerful message of the grace of God for others who had to suffer. He was used to lead many to the Saviour.

ಬಂಣ

It was not long before Jemari wanted to join us at Giyu to reach the Bodis. But, when he arrived, Jemari was dismayed to find that most of the Bodi warriors towered over him in height. Many of the women were also much taller. He found that the Bodis were aggressive, belligerent and threatening. They laughed at the short man and said that they would soon "eat him." Jemari had never seen such cruel, evil men and he was very afraid of them. The way the warriors drank warm blood from their cows quite sickened him.

Jemari wished he could be like Tekka and Nana. They were fearless and determined and they were trusting God to work among the Bodi people. But, day after day, as he heard threats and rumours about plans to kill him, Jemari's fear only increased. He could not sleep at night. He could not eat and he jumped at every strange sound. He stayed near the house where we lived and went inside if any of the young warriors came around carrying weapons. I guess Jemari had 'culture shock.' He couldn't believe he was still in Ethiopia!

Soon Jemari complained of being sick, but had no definite symptoms — no fever, no pain. Nana, Tekka and I often prayed with Jemari and encouraged him to trust the Lord for his safety. Nana counselled him every day. Tekka told Jemari how he also had been afraid of the Bodis and how the Lord had delivered him from that fear.

But Jemari only got worse.

He was ashamed of his fear, but couldn't seem to face it or to deal with it. We all felt sorry for Jemari. We prayed and longed to help him. But, he became thin and listless and we feared that soon he really would become sick. Jemari became a real burden on the whole team, as he wanted someone always to be with him. He would not even take his turn in going to the spring for water or to the bush for firewood unless one of us accompanied him. We all wanted to help Jemari, but nothing we said or did seemed to help.

Finally we decided to send Jemari home. Maybe back in his own environment, among his own family and friends, he would recover. We wanted him to again be the useful worker he had been. Very early one morning, long before the Bodis were aware of it, we sent Jemari off home to Mallo. Tekka accompanied him as far as Dimae and some Dimae believers went with him the rest of the way. We all thought that would be the last we would see of Jemari.

༄༅༄

For weeks we were busy cutting down the tall elephant grass to clear a thousand metre long airstrip for the Missionary Aviation Fellowship (MAF) aeroplane. It was really hard work in the blazing sun. We cleared some more land for places to build a clinic and a school. We also trekked to nearby villages to share the Gospel message as many people kept asking to hear "The Jesus Story."

One night as the five evangelists and I sat around the fire and talked and prayed together, Tekka asked about the Bodi people who lived further down the valley at Gura. They were the same tribe, but a different clan from the Shirim among whom we lived at Giyu. We heard that Gura was the place where all the cattle were kept that had been stolen from Konta across the Omo River. As we prayed for all the Bodi clans: Shirim, Gura, Hanna and Goldiya, Tekka was especially burdened for the Gura clan and poured out his heart for those people. They were only a few hours walk away.

A week later Tekka told us that he believed God wanted him to go and tell the Bodis at Gura about Jesus. The team decided that I should go with him — just the two of us. It could be very dangerous. The other evangelists would stay at Giyu to keep witnessing to the Bodis who came to visit and to pray for us.

༄༅

But first, somehow, we had to get food to some evangelists among the Mursi tribe to the south. Mahae was there with two young Wolaitta evangelists who had their wives and young children with them. The MAF aircraft had regularly supplied them, but the communist government grounded all the MAF and the other mission planes. Some evangelists were left in remote places waiting in vain for their food and medical supplies. They could get very little locally and were getting desperate. They waited and longed for the aeroplanes to come with their food supplies, not knowing why they could not come.

Nor could they get out. A flooded river had cut them off.. Mahae and his friends were totally isolated. They used up all their food. The children cried with hunger and the adults prayed for help. Mahae found some wild honey and some berries, roots and leaves that they could eat.

೮೦೦೪

Going by a roundabout way I was able to join Bark Fahnestock from our mission station at Bako. We tried to drive into Mursi through the Mago Valley, but couldn't get through. The road had been closed to vehicles for years and tall grass had obliterated the track. We had to return to the town of Jinka. Bark went back up the mountain to his home at Bako. We would keep in touch by radio.

Filling up the vehicle's fuel tanks, I took two young Ethiopian men and tried again, this time with a lighter load. Bediru said he knew the road, but down in the Mago Valley, he also got us lost! For two days we struggled through the tall grass, but again we had to turn back. It was so frustrating. Then we ran out of water! Then the radio would not work properly. Then I became violently sick and Bediru had a high fever too. It was one thing after another! Eventually we got a brief radio message through to Bako.

The next morning, Bark set out with mules to help us. Despite a terrible headache and fever, I was able to drive us back out of the valley. We had almost reached Jinka town when Bark met us. What a welcome sight he was!

Leaving the vehicle in Jinka, we rode the mules up the mountain to Bako. Bediru and I were both laid low with malaria. MAF was given permission for an emergency flight to fly me out to Addis Ababa. It was weeks before I was well enough to return to Giyu with food supplies. With some Christian volunteer carriers from Dimae, I trekked through the hot valley with grain for Mahae and the others in Mursi.

But, while I was away recovering in Addis Ababa, our appointed day for the trip to Gura arrived. Tekka set off alone for Gura. He never returned. He was ambushed and killed as he took the Gospel of Christ to those darkened Bodi people.

                          ಬಿಡ

Then suddenly, 'out of the blue,' Jemari returned! From his home in Mallo, he had walked, all alone, through Basketo and Dimae, then through Bodi territory, all the way to Giyu! What a surprise it was to see him. He gave a great shout and announced that he had come to take Tekka's place! Jemari was so changed that we hardly knew him. From the 'scared little rabbit' of a few months before, he came laughing, fearless and rejoicing in the Lord's strength. I asked Jemari whatever had happened to change him.

That evening as we sat around the smoky fire, Jemari told us his story. What a testimony it was! When news of Tekka's death reached him, Jemari started to shake again and cry. He went out alone into the woods on the mountain near his home. He went there to meet the Lord. He confessed his fear, his weakness. And he asked God to take the fear right out of his heart. Jemari told the Lord that he couldn't go on as he was and he pleaded for deliverance.

Jemari smiled at us. "Suddenly a peace I had never known before swept over me," he said. "The load was lifted off me. I felt such joy. Ever since I have been at peace. Praise God, the fear has gone." Jemari fairly beamed at us and we all rejoiced with him. How different he was now when he prayed — his whole vision and purpose were different — he felt he was safe in God's hands and had nothing to lose.

                          ಬಿಡ

From that day on, Jemari was absolutely fearless. He went openly and alone to the Bodi houses. The people were amazed at the change in the little man. They always admired courage. Jemari went alone to places where some others of us hesitated to go. He went to the Gura clan and beyond

Hanna. It was Jemari who finally found out the truth about Tekka's death. He located the place of the murder and was able to identify the killer.

Jemari shared the Gospel of Christ with hundreds of Bodi people. He sat outside their small huts or under the shady trees among the warriors. He told and retold the story of God's great love in giving His Son to bear our sins and to die for us. He spoke loudly so the women in the huts and nearby fields could hear too! He played with the children and told them stories about Jesus. In every way Jemari took Tekka's place.

Jemari worked closely with Nana. When the communist authorities closed down the mission stations, most of the evangelists were also forced out of the areas where they worked. In March 1977 I left Giyu and soon afterwards, the communist cadres hunted all of the evangelists out of the Bodi area. Jemari and Nana returned to Mallo, but often they went back to Dimae for short visits where they were able to contact a few Bodis who came to the monthly market there.

Now twenty-five years later, Jemari is the coordinator of all the Mallo evangelists and recently took some of these young evangelists to the Dimae and Bodi tribes. He led a group of thirty Dimae Christians to Hanna town where they cleared the old, neglected airstrip. Jemari still travels the narrow trails through Dimae and Bodi country sharing the Good News. He is always encouraging and teaching the new believers, establishing new churches, helping the persecuted Christians and building up the kingdom of Christ. His wife and family in Mallo support him as he *"endures hardship as a good soldier of Jesus Christ."*

EPILOGUE

In January 2005 I drove again to Dimae Gero. I had met Jemari there before and I was anticipating another great reunion. However, just before I arrived, I was told that Jemari had died of fever. Was it malaria? I never did find out. Jemari was buried in Mallo where his wife Telimito still lives. Some of his children are still in school, but several older ones are active in Christian service. One is a pastor in one of the Bulki town churches. Telimito needs prayer for the Lord's protection as an evil neighbour who persecuted Jemari, has threatened to kill her. He tried unsuccessfully once. He wants to steal the land that Jemari and Nana cleared out of the bush for their homes and crops.

So another humble, faithful evangelist has gone to his reward — by God's grace to rejoice forever in the presence of his Lord and Saviour. The little, enthusiastic, energetic evangelist was a great help and encouragement to me during my *"journeys oft"* in the Omo River Valley. I miss him deeply and thank God for the privilege of knowing and serving with him in the Gospel of Christ. When the story of the Bodi warriors and their contact with, and their response to, the Gospel of Christ is written, no name will shine brighter than that of Jemari, the little evangelist who let the Lord take away his fearful heart and give him the heart of a lion!

14

NANA

An Unusual Prayer
ಬ♣ಐ

I sought the Lord and He answered me; He delivered me from all my fears... This poor man called, and the Lord heard him and saved him out of all his troubles... The young lions grow weak and hungry; but those who seek the Lord lack no good thing.

Psalm 34:4, 6 & 10

"I ask this in the name of Your Son, our Saviour, the Lord Jesus Christ. Amen." We started to rise to our feet at the end of our prayer time, but then Evangelist Nana added a bit more, a postscript, on the end of his prayer, "O Lord, when we go down the valley tomorrow, let us see a lion. Amen." Six sets of eyes, the other evangelists and mine, all stared at Nana.

ಬಐ

At Giyu in Bodi, the six evangelists and I had shared our evening devotions as usual. We read some Bible verses and claimed one of the precious promises or discussed the Lord's commands we saw in the Scripture passage. Then kneeling on our hands and knees with our foreheads on the dirt floor, we had all prayed. Nana then tacked on the extra sentence!

"That was a strange thing to pray for," I said, "Why did you ask to see a lion?"

Nana simply replied, "Because I have never seen one and I would like to."

The next day Nana, Desta, Matusel and I were planning to trek to Gura where our brother evangelist Tekka had been killed about two months earlier. We had just found out the area where he had been murdered and the name of the young man who killed him. We hoped to go on to Bodi cattle camps along the Omo River and return past the police post at Hanna. It was near the end of a very long Dry Season and terribly hot — the worst time to travel — but there never seemed to be a best time! At least there would not be as many tsetse flies or malarial mosquitoes because it was so dry. The grazing lands had all dried off to dust and most of the water holes were also dry. The Bodi herdsmen took their cattle down to the Omo River where some grass and reeds grew along the banks of the river. It was the unbearable heat, the sun reflecting off the rocks, the dust, the sticky flies, the thorn bushes, the weariness and the unknown, the uncertainties that bothered me. And now Nana wanted a lion!

I said to Nana, "But you have seen lions, haven't you." Many nights at Giyu lions chased zebras right past our grass huts and in the morning we saw their paw prints in the dust outside our doors.

Nana replied, "No, I have never seen a lion. I hear them roaring or hunting the deer and zebras. I have seen the tall grass waving as they hunt, but I have never seen one."

This I found hard to believe. The province where we worked was called *Gamo Gofa* ~ lion and mane of the lion, but somehow Nana had missed them. I told him of several times when lions had crossed my path as I travelled by mule and of a lion that killed a calf at Zala and carried it off, only twenty metres from me. Then I told him how lions tried to chase off my mule when Tekka and I spent a miserable night in the tall grass halfway between Basketo and Dimae and how we had to keep a fire going all night to keep them away. All of us had seen lions when we flashed our torches at night at Giyu, but not Nana.

One time we nearly lost our daughter Mimi to lions by the Mazi River. We were digging our 4WD Land Rover out of the mud. We had been stuck for hours and after a while Mimi wandered off in the twilight down towards the river. When lions started coughing in the grass nearby, we just had time to yell, chase and grab Mimi and race with her back to the car. We started the engine, turned on the lights and tooted the horn to scare off the lions! But, Nana still wanted to see a lion! So I said, "May the Lord grant your prayer," and we all went to sleep.

ಐಂಜ

Months before Evangelist Mahae had purchased a mule for me to take to Bodi, but it had little chance of survival there because of the tsetse flies that carried sleeping sickness. I was able to have some medicine flown in from Europe and with monthly injections we were able to keep the mule there for six months. While we walked everywhere, the mule carried our food, medicines, spare clothes and water canteens.

The first day we walked eighteen kilometres from Giyu to a waterhole near Hanna where we filled up all the containers. Altogether we had thirteen metal canteens and a five litre plastic container of water. This was the last water supply we knew about, but we hoped to find some more at Gura. It was just so hot at this time of the year — both by day and night. By mid morning we found it hard to stay together. We had to keep stopping for Nana to catch up as he walked increasingly slower. In the relentless heat most of the water was used up. By late afternoon we needed to find another waterhole —

and fast! The mule was exhausted and dropped its head lower and lower to the ground.

Every water hole we came to was dry and each creek bed just dry rocks. Every village was deserted and the cattle corrals empty. It seemed the people had all gone down to the Omo River. There were no trails to follow and we stumbled on — that is the best way to describe our journey through the thorn bushes. We spent an uncomfortable night and the next day was even hotter — one of the worst days of my life. The water was all gone and we were too far from the waterhole at Hanna to return there. We were desperate and cried out to the Lord for help.

Then Nana collapsed! He just passed out at my feet and it took us several minutes to revive him. We helped him up and went forward, but soon he collapsed again. The burning noontime sun was too much for us all. Even the mule was staggering and lay in a heap while we rested for a couple of hours in the poor shade of a bush. Nana said he could not go any further and that we should leave him there and return for him when we found water. None of us agreed to that — we had to stay together — we would never have found him again out there in that bush. We went on a distance further and I helped Nana along, holding him up by the back of his trousers. Then Nana went down again and it took us a long time to revive him.

Up ahead was a small hill. Desta pointed to it with his chin and said if we climbed it we would see over the grass and thorn bushes to a village or a waterhole. By this time we were all exhausted. I knew I didn't have the strength to climb that rise and I doubted if the others had either. All our lips were cracked, our mouths dry and it was hard to breathe, let alone talk. Then Nana collapsed again. I let him down onto the ground and prayed. The Lord knew how desperate we were! When Nana recovered, we lifted him up. I shuffled along close behind him, holding him up.

༄༅

We went another short distance and walked right into the middle of a pride of lions! I don't know who got the biggest shock — the lions or us! The lions had been sleeping under the bushes out of the sun. There were ten lions — two big males, two very small cubs and the rest females. The two little cubs rushed up to us and started sniffing at the mule. The mule just froze! It went stiff legged, its tail horizontal, eyes staring, ears straight up and mouth wide open! It had never seen lions before and the lions had never seen a mule before either.

Nana froze in mid stride, front foot in the air, arms wide and eyes as large as saucers! When the adult lions saw their cubs near the mule, they went into protective mode. They rose up, roared loudly and charged us from three sides. Nana was just petrified with one foot in the air!

I was terrified too! My feet were stuck on the ground and would not move. Somehow, suddenly, I found two large rocks in my hands, but I have no idea how they got there! I bobbed up and down like a demented ostrich with the rocks in my hands, but my feet were glued to the ground and would not shift! The other evangelists screamed and struggled to get the machete that was tied on the mule with the water canteens. The pack of lions was now up in the air, roaring and coming to tear us apart and we couldn't move!

The terrified mule saved us! Frozen stiff, legs apart, it just seemed to levitate. It rose up a metre into the air. Then it came crashing down and the empty water canteens rattled and banged together with a frightful racket. The cubs were scared out of their wits and they raced away back past the charging lions. The awful noise and the cubs rushing the other way stopped the lions in mid flight. Some turned in mid air and some came through, over, past us still roaring and slashing the air with their sharp claws. Somehow (only by the mercy and grace of God) they missed us and in a few seconds they all disappeared into the bush.

For a few seconds we just stood there transfixed. Nana still had his foot in the air, arms askew, and eyes wide. My feet were still stuck on the ground, but I dropped the rocks. Then absolute pandemonium broke loose! Nana, who supposedly could not take another step, just took off! He raced up the hill and reached the top in about a minute. I was right behind him! The mule passed both of us halfway up and the other evangelists made it a 'blanket finish.'

We all collapsed on the ground. I said, "Nana, the Lord surely answered your prayer!"

He replied, "Yes, truly, God heard and answered my prayer." Then the reaction suddenly set in! We started laughing. For about ten minutes we laughed and laughed! We laughed until it hurt. We laughed and we cried and rolled on the ground. I guess we were all just hysterical with relief. When we recovered and lay gasping on the ground, I reached across, grabbed Nana's thigh and growled loudly.

Nana jumped and shouted "*Anbessa* ~ Lion!" The other evangelists sat bolt upright and Desta grabbed for the machete. Then we laughed again! We talked about lions for days afterwards!

ಬಂಡ

When we looked over the thorn bushes, all we could see were empty corrals and abandoned villages, but no water, except the Omo River far off in the distance. The mule wandered off, sniffing the air and about fifty metres away, found a pool. I can't say it was a pool of water! In a hollow in a flat rock, thick, green slime covered some liquid — we could not call it H_2O. There was evidence that baboons and leopards had been there a long time ago. It may not have been more than 20% water, but to us it was just like nectar! We drank it eagerly and swallowed a water-purifying tablet afterwards! We knew it was the Lord's provision and it saved our lives. We were so grateful and praised God together. Even the mule drank some, as it was so thirsty.

We came down off the hill rejoicing — stumbling, still weak and shaky — but rejoicing. Towards evening we found a Bodi warrior out hunting. He told Desta he heard lions roaring and asked if we had seen them. Had we seen them? We sure had! The hunter led us to a spring of water hidden among the rocks in a ravine. What a time we had there — drinking water, boiling tea, washing ourselves, filling the canteens and drinking some more! How we rejoiced and praised God for His goodness! We stayed the night at the spring, sleeping on the flat rocks near the water. Nobody wanted to be far from the water. Before we slept, Nana thanked God for the lions! The rest of us thanked the Lord for the liquid on the hill and for the water at the spring — especially for the water!

15

DESTA

Names are Important
༅ ❁ ༄

Those who know Your Name will trust in you, for you, Lord, have never forsaken those who trust in you.
Psalm 9:10

They will call on My Name and I will answer them; I will say, "They are My people," and they will say, "The LORD is our GOD."
Zechariah 13:9

It was with much praise to God and with a huge sense of relief that evangelists Desta, Nana, Matusel and I stumbled down off the hill in Gura. Then we 'just happened to find' a Bodi warrior who was out hunting. For half an hour he led us through the bush to a nice spring of clear water flowing out of the rocks. Here we were able to drink all we wanted! We were all hot, feverish, totally exhausted and terribly thirsty! Because the sun had set and it was quickly getting dark, the Bodi hunter hurriedly left us and disappeared into the bush. I wondered where he went, but I was totally exhausted and could not even think straight. All I wanted to do was to drink the cool water and then, to drink some more! All of the evangelists were the same.

After we drank our fill and washed ourselves, we got on our knees and prayed together. All I could do was whisper, "Thank You, Lord," over and over again. Nana then prayed and thanked God for the lions that caused us to run up the hill. Desta praised the Lord for the small amount of 'fluid' we found up there that saved our lives and for the Bodi hunter who showed us the way to the spring. We would never have found it by ourselves. The spring was hidden among the rocks in a ravine. Desta also praised the Lord for the cool water — especially for the water!

As we sat around the fire for a little while that night, most of the talk was about lions! We kept the fire going all night so they did not visit us again! On that terrible journey we did not find the place where Tekka was killed — it was not important to do so, and it would be a long time before we did find it. But, we prayed that we might find what Tekka went after — souls lost in darkness, sin and fear — souls for whom Christ died. We realised afresh that:

> *we wrestle against the authorities, against the powers of this dark world and against the spiritual forces of evil.*
>
> Ephesians 6:12

Like Tekka, we wanted to share the Good News about Christ, the Water of Life, with some Bodi people. We asked the Lord to lead us to them.

ಬಿಡಿ

As the sun rose next morning, the Bodi warrior returned as suddenly as he had gone. He invited us to come to his village. He said it was not too far away, just a little further down the ravine. The people crowded around us when we arrived. And there we met Lushinda, the oldest Bodi man we had seen! He had been the chief of his clan, but was now old and stiff with arthritis. His body bore many scars from wounds sustained in raids on other tribes. Along his arms were rows of raised lumps — ω shapes — that were made by cutting the skin and inserting small pieces of charcoal. Each lump represented a man of another tribe that he had killed in battle. I lost count after a hundred lumps! As Lushinda was no longer able to lead the warriors into battle, his son replaced him as chief of the clan. He protected Lushinda from the threats of many young warriors who were keen 'to drink Lushinda's blood to get his strength and courage.'

Lushinda was very attentive as we gave the Gospel message. He sat enthralled at the stories we told the people about the Lord Jesus. Desta interpreted for us as we related several of the parables Jesus told. We told them some of His wonderful healing miracles, but we always finished with the greatest story — that of His death and resurrection. Never before had Lushinda and his people heard the name of Jesus Christ. For some hours Lushinda listened carefully to the message about sin and repentance, of God's love and forgiveness, of peace and eternal life — the free gift we could receive. He asked us many questions and as is the custom of the Bodi tribe, Lushinda discussed each of the stories with the other men of the village.

Lushinda responded eagerly to the invitation to "walk the Jesus road." He confessed his sin and renounced Satan, blood sacrifices and spirit worship. Holding both hands high Lushinda accepted Jesus as his Saviour. We rejoiced and praised God that we had found him before it was too late. But, I wondered how much Lushinda really understood. It was all so new! Thank the Lord that He knows for He looks on the heart. It takes little faith to receive God's wonderful gift of salvation in Christ.

Before we left, we taught Lushinda to pray and said he should do that every day because the Bible says:

> *Whoever calls on the Name of the LORD shall be saved.*
>
> Romans 10:13

We wished that we could stay longer in that village, but we needed to go on further. We committed Lushinda to God's care and hoped that one day soon two evangelists could come and live in his village and teach him more of the Scriptures.

ಔಓ

One behind the other, we found our way through the tall grass and thorn bushes and reached the top of the ridge. Then we heard someone calling out. A man was calling us from the Bodi village that we had just left in the ravine, about a kilometre away. It was old Lushinda. He was calling out, "Tell me His Name again! His name. His Name. Tell me His name again. I might forget."

Desta and I stood together and in unison, shouted back, "His name is *Eyesus Kiristos* ~ Jesus Christ. His name is Jesus. Pray to Jesus."

Up from the village, a breeze carried Lushinda's reply, "Yes, His name is Jesus Christ. I will call to Him. I won't forget."

That journey was one of the most difficult and it nearly ended in disaster, but it became one of the most fruitful. For a long time afterwards Nana dreamed of lions. I dreamed of an old man calling out, "Tell me His Name again."

> *Everyone who calls on the Name of the Lord will be saved. How, then, can they call on the one they have not believed in? And how can they believe in the one of whom they have not heard? And how can they hear without someone preaching to them? And how can they preach unless they are sent? As it is written, 'How beautiful are the feet of those who bring Good News!*
>
> Romans 10:13-15

16

FANTA

An Unlikely Candidate
ಬ✽ಜ

Not many wise, not many influential and powerful, not many of high and noble birth are called, but God deliberately chose the foolish, the weak, the insignificant, the despised, the 'nothings,' that no one should boast in the presence of God.

1 Corinthians 1:26-28

"Sit down, young man. Sit down. You cannot go. Sit down."

The church pastor leading the meeting waved to the man to sit down. But, he remained standing, leaning on a stout walking stick, looking around confused, not understanding. An older church elder called out to him, "Fanta. Wait. Just sit down now." The young man sat down in the crowd.

ಬಜ

It happened at a District Convention among the Wolaitta people. Several thousand Christians had gathered for their annual Bible conference. For five days we had a precious time together studying God's Word and praising the Lord in song and testimony. It was my privilege to give several messages during the meetings. One of these was the missionary challenge when I called for young men and women to leave their home area and go as national missionaries to take the Gospel to other tribes.

Some people call these men "evangelists," and they surely are that, but they are just as much "missionaries" as we are who come from the Western world. They leave their own ethnic group, travel hundreds of kilometres and live among diverse people groups. Where necessary they live in different types of houses, learn new languages, eat some different foods, adjust to strange cultures and customs and humbly live a peaceful, joyous life-style that causes their neighbours to enquire why they are not afraid, as they are themselves. 'friendship evangelism' opens up many contacts to share the Good News of salvation through Christ.

Standing in the centre of the people who had circled all around the stand, I called for young people to give themselves to Christ for His service. Sitting nearby were the pastors and elders, the leaders of the churches. They were the ones who would eventually interview any who came forward. They would examine each candidate carefully and send some back to receive Bible School training or to get more preaching experience. They would send others out immediately if they thought they were ready for the hardships ahead. About twenty young folk came forward to say they would go out as cross-cultural missionaries.

Then Fanta stood up and called out that he would also go. The leaders told him to sit down. He stood there holding on to his stick. I soon discovered why the elders rejected him. Fanta was a cripple! He had only been about six years of age when he had a stroke. Perhaps it was polio, meningitis, cerebral malaria or some other disease that caused it, but it left him completely paralysed down the right side of his body and crooked in stature. There was nobody in the area to give Fanta the medical treatment and specialised care he needed. His family had no money to take him to the city either.

So, he grew up misshapen, handicapped, with a withered, useless arm and leg. They just hung at his side. Fortunately his face recovered and he was able to speak clearly and sing beautifully. His leg was a nuisance. Fanta just dragged it behind him. To move, he stood on his left leg that was very strong and moved his stick ahead a pace. Then he hopped forward, dragging his right leg, and when he caught his balance, he did it again, and again! It wasn't a pretty sight. It took Fanta a long time to get anywhere. So he wasn't much of a candidate. We wanted strong men who could walk hundreds of kilometres over rough mountain trails.

Without stopping to think or pray, I moved over to the young man and repeated what the elders had said — that Fanta could not be an evangelist. I suggested that he could have a ministry of prayer. However, Fanta interrupted me. "That is what the elders said two years ago when I asked them. They told me to go to Bible School and learn. So I went and completed the course. Now I am ready to go. God's Word burns in my heart. I want to go to the cattle herders along the Bilate River and near Lake Abaya. I know they are the enemies of the Wolaitta people, but they need Jesus too. God has called me to go to them. Please ask the elders again to send me," he pleaded.

I found out later that Fanta had graduated at the top of his class. Now he pointed with his chin to the hot lowlands and said that the Lord wanted him to take the Gospel of Christ down there to the cattle herders. When I told him that the Oromo clan killed all outsiders — near the lake they had murdered the evangelist Omochi, the husband of Baloti who worked with Vida in women's conferences — he was undeterred and seemingly unafraid. He couldn't run away, nor could he stand and fight either! "God has told me to go, so I must obey," he said. He asked me to pray for him and also to intercede with the elders again on his behalf. Then slowly he hopped away on his stick. I am always amazed at the grace, the patience and the long-suffering of the Lord. His ways are so different to mine! He makes no mistakes and moves for our good at just the right moment. Sometimes He must grieve at my stupidity and my lack of faith and trust!

๛ග

A year later I met Fanta again, the missionary candidate we had rejected. Fanta was so sure that the Lord had called him that he went alone into the lowlands by Lake Abaya. None of the other candidates was able to go there. The area Fanta went to was two days walk away — for the average person, that is! It took Fanta five long days to get there. Sometimes he fell and he was a bit scratched and bruised when he arrived. He found the semi-nomadic clan had large herds of cattle that they guarded jealously. The warriors were dangerous and their fierce reputation as killers of all outsiders was correct. Few would go near that tribe — they killed strangers, no questions asked.

But, this young man, compelled by the love of Christ, went down to them. Fanta really had nothing to lose. The Lord had called him and had He not promised to go with those whom He sent? If those savage warriors killed him, he would go to be with his Lord. Then Fanta discovered an amazing thing about these cattle herders that was different from all the other tribes around. They honoured cripples! Maybe there had been, in generations past, an awful epidemic — polio maybe — that had left many people in the tribe as cripples. None of the other tribes in that area seemed to have any handicapped or deformed children around as they leave them to die, usually of starvation.

Directed by the Spirit of God, Fanta had found the only tribe where he could safely go and no one else could! The tribe actually accepted, welcomed and respected him. It was no problem for him to live among them. He was able to hop from one village to another and to the cattle camps and tell the Gospel story over and over again. It took him a long time, but he visited all the camps. The Lord powerfully blessed his witness and he started churches in five villages!

Within a year at least 250 people had believed the Gospel and accepted Christ as their Saviour. Many of them came to the next convention with Fanta and I met them there. They came; some women dressed in bark skirts and cowhide aprons; some men in animal skins and carrying their weapons. They came singing chants of praise to Jesus Christ. They all walked slowly to keep pace with their leader who hopped along on one leg and a stick. I marvelled again at the grace of God and thanked Him that He uses any person, no matter what handicap they have, if they love and obey Him. The elders accepted the rejected candidate at last!

The Wolaitta church leaders soon sent another national missionary to help Fanta teach the new Christians. They asked me to preach at the first Baptismal Service when twenty-eight believers were baptised in the Bilate River near the place where it flows into Lake Abaya. A curious crowd of armed warriors stood on the other side of the river and watched the proceedings. On our side of the river a group of teenagers kept throwing large rocks into the river to keep the crocodiles away from the baptismal site.

Today in that clan of the Oromo tribe there are more than twenty churches. Young men have been trained in Bible School for leadership positions and some are pastors to their own people. Others have gone to other groups to tell the story of Jesus Christ. Fanta, now with a wife and family, still serves the Lord faithfully in that area where, at that time, no one but he could go.

How awesome, how wonderful, how powerful, how loving is our God! He is all knowing and He makes no blunders. He equips His people for just the right ministry in exactly the right place. He uses ordinary people who serve Him faithfully to bring Him the honour and praise that is His due. Lord, give us more of your special, weak, handicapped servants!

17

TASSEW

Tortured for Christ

ಬ✽ಲ

Others were tortured and refused to be released (by denying their faith), so that they might gain a better resurrection.
Hebrews 11:35

Finally, let no one cause me trouble, for I bear on my body the marks of the Lord Jesus (the brand of ownership).
Galatians 6:17

That day started like so many before it. Their mother awakened her teenage sons, Tassew and Tanga early, at first light. She stoked up the fire and soon had coffee boiling and some roasted corn ready for their breakfast. Tassew helped Tanga get his clothes on while Tanga complained of the pain in his arms and legs. They were older than their six siblings who were still asleep on their palm-leaf mats on the dirt floors of some of the other houses.

That day their father Hebana was with one of his other wives in the circle of six houses that made up his compound. Hebana was known as a proud, angry and violent man who should not be 'crossed.' He was also known as the most powerful witchdoctor in that part of Wolaitta. It was said that he had the powers of *Shaitan* ~ Satan and the *budda* ~ evil eye to discern the guilty party in any dispute. He could bring sickness and death to any who failed to bring him suitable gifts and sacrifices for the spirits of the ancestors. He dispensed traditional potions made from herbs, roots, leaves and berries for sores and wounds. But, Hebana could do nothing to heal his own son who grew weaker and more sickly as the weeks and months passed. The pain in Tanga's body grew worse day by day and nothing seemed to help.

Tanga grabbed extra pieces of corn for their midday snack while Tassew released the mule, donkeys, cows and goats from their stalls around the walls and chased them out of the house. The warm sun rose as the boys drove the animals from the six houses out to the grazing land. Tanga limped slowly behind Tassew. The sores on his feet were getting worse and he found it difficult to walk. Tanga had contracted the dreaded leprosy and already had open sores not only on his feet, but also on his face and body. His hands were deformed and numb and his ears, nose and lips were infected. He found it hard to swallow. Unless he received treatment soon, he was sure to die. Neither his father nor anyone else knew of medicine that could help leprosy. So Tanga just got worse each day.

That day seemed like any other as Tassew and Tanga sat for awhile in the sun, then in the shade, watching the animals graze. They did not know how their lives and that of their family and their community would change that day forever! Tassew gathered two bundles of sticks as he did each day to carry home for their mother's fire. He wished he could help his brother more, but he did not know what to do. So the boys sat together on the hillside as they did every day.

༄༅

Then they saw a man coming across the fields towards them. Chando walked with a bad limp as he came up from the lowlands towards the boys. Barely 150 centimetres tall (five feet), his head was permanently inclined to one side and he was very hard of hearing. He was one of the 'running preachers' who survived the oppressive Italian occupation. These dozen men were sometimes called the 'night preachers' because they ran through the dark night, awakened a village about midnight to preach the Gospel of

Christ. They taught the new converts, but before dawn began running again towards home or for a safe hiding place in the forest. The next night they ran in a different direction to another village and repeated the message. They returned later at night to teach the converts and to baptise them in a river.

The Italian soldiers hunted these brave evangelists and put a price on their heads. Some of them were caught and killed. Others severely punished and imprisoned. Some were betrayed for the reward. All suffered great hardship. Only a few survived the war without some permanent physical damage. We were privileged to know three and to work with two of these great 'running preachers.' Chando had also been captured, kicked and beaten about the head and neck with a rifle butt, then imprisoned for a year. The beating destroyed his hearing, left him with a limp and a damaged neck that gave him continual pain.

Tassew and Tanga watched Chando as he approached. He greeted them with a cry of *"Serro! Serro!* ~ Peace! Peace" He sat down on a rock and said, "I have a wonderful story to tell you. It is a true story about *Eyesus Kiristos* ~ Jesus Christ, the Son of God, the great Creator. The story is in this book." As Tassew and Tanga watched, Chando pulled from his bag a battered old Bible that he opened and started to read aloud. Time seemed to stand still as Chando told the boys about Jesus, his life, death and resurrection. Several hours passed as Tassew and Tanga listened enthralled to "the old, old story" of God's grace, of redemption and forgiveness of sin, of new life and a home in Heaven. It was the first time they heard the name of Jesus.

Tassew asked Chando what it would cost to have eternal life and to follow Jesus. He had to shout the question twice into Chando's ear to make him hear. Chando smiled as he replied, "Nothing and everything. It costs nothing, because it is a free gift that God gives to those who believe. You have to renounce Satan and his ways, accept Jesus in your heart as Saviour and Lord. And, it also costs everything because some will oppose you and there may be suffering for those who follow Jesus with a full heart. 'A man has two legs, but he can only climb one centre-pole at a time'." Wolaitta houses were round, beehive shaped with a large centre-pole holding up a framework of poles tied together with vines. A thick grass thatch came down to within a few centimetres of the ground and provided good insulation from both the cold and the heat. Each house had only one centre-pole, so the saying meant, "You can only be in one house at a time — so choose which house you want to belong to!"

As the shadows lengthened, both Tassew and Tanga said they believed and would follow the Lord Jesus. Out on the hillside they shouted out their renunciation of Satan and their acceptance of Christ — 'with two hands' — completely, full surrender. Chando taught the boys to pray every morning and night and before they ate their food. He went with them as they drove the animals home. Chando tried to talk to the boys' father, but Hebana flew into a rage and drove him out of the compound. He had plans for Tassew to become the next witchdoctor in the long family line, but Tassew was not interested as the blood sacrifices and 'medicines,' while the 'potions' his father made, seemed only to make Tanga worse.

൞ഗ

And now the brothers had peace and joy in their new faith and bubbled over in happiness. They had life now and a home with Jesus in Heaven! That night when Hebana came into the house and asked them about Chando, Tassew and Tanga, in the excitement of their new faith, told their father what Chando had said to them. They told how they had believed in Jesus Christ, God's son and from now on were "walking the Jesus Road."

Hebana went berserk! He grabbed Tassew and tied him to the centre pole of the house with ropes used to tether animals near the house. His mother protested, but was abused and pushed away. Hebana whipped Tassew severely and demanded he deny "this Jesus." Despite the pain of his bleeding back, Tassew just shook his head. He would not go back on his commitment to Christ. This drove Hebana into an absolute fury! He took a sickle from the wall and put the metal in the fire. As he waited for it to heat, he turned on Tanga to abuse and curse him. When he tried to hit Tanga, his mother stood over their sickly son to protect him.

Then he took the red-hot sickle and pressed it onto Tassew's legs. The smell of his burning legs and the excruciating pain made Tassew cry out, but he kept refusing to reject the Saviour. He received a dozen long burns across his legs before he passed out and his body sagged in the ropes tying him to the pole. His brother's cries of "Stop! Stop!" were heard all over the compound and beyond. His mother gave the shrill distress cry and it brought the family and neighbours running and shouting. Hebana was beside himself, but allowed men take the sickle and to push him outside while others cut Tassew free. Tassew was laid on the bamboo mat. His mother bathed his face and when he was conscious, gave him water to drink. She rubbed butter on his burns and salt water on the stripes on his back. It was weeks before Tassew's wounds healed and he was free of pain.

Tassew and Tanga prayed together and told the Gospel stories to their mother and the other family members in the other houses. The neighbours soon heard them too. Their father had disappeared into the forest for weeks to consult the powers of darkness. The brothers told everyone the Bible stories they heard from Chando. They started going to the surrounding villages and sharing the Good News.

ಬಿಲ್

While Tassew grew bigger and stronger, Tanga got weaker and weaker. Soon Tanga could no longer walk, so Tassew carried him on his back. He made a kind of bag for his brother to sit in with straps Tassew tied over his shoulders. That was the way women carried their loads of firewood, their water pots and loads of grain. Some people laughed at the young men, but Tassew did not mind. He was happy to carry his brother. Tassew had to do all the talking because Tanga could not talk properly. Tanga prayed in a mumble as Tassew told of God's love in Christ. Many men and women were listening to the Gospel and some said they wanted to believe. The evangelist Chando returned occasionally to accompany them and teach them more of God's Word. Soon people started to believe; an elderly couple, two farmers, some women and a family. Within two years about twenty small groups of believers were meeting regularly for worship in the *selot bet* ~ prayer houses they built in their villages.

One night Tanga died quietly in his sleep. He had fallen asleep on Tassew's back as they travelled home from a distant village. He did not want to eat the soft food their mother had prepared. She was a Christian now and prayed with her boys before they ate. Tanga was so tired. Tired and happy. He tried to smile and lay down on his mat and went to sleep. He woke up in the arms of Jesus.

Tassew preached the Gospel at Tanga's funeral to the hundreds of people who gathered. Chando and other evangelists came to help organise the funeral, but they let Tassew give the message of God's love and grace, of forgiveness of sin and reconciliation. Hebana just sat with the family and watched the Christian funeral. He knew his power was broken. He had lost the control that he had held over the people for so long.

ಬಂಡ

Soon Tassew had the joy of leading his witchdoctor father to Christ. The family had a great bonfire in the centre of the compound to burn all the satanic charms, potions, and poisons and the *Shaitan bet* ~ Satan house itself, the *adaba* ~ sacred tree where they worshipped the spirits of their ancestors and the altar — everything to do with their old life. What a time of rejoicing it was that day! Hebana became a humble follower of Jesus Christ and eventually he was made a leader in the church. All of his children became Christians too and he made sure that his daughters married Christian young men.

Tassew's brother Samuel became one of the main church elders in Wolaitta and served with us in Bolosso and Soddo for many years. He still serves the Lord, leading the churches and supporting the evangelists, more of whom went out from Bolosso than from any other district of Wolaitta. A younger brother Markos became a Bible School teacher with us at Bolosso, a convention speaker and for a time, an evangelist among the Muslim Arsi people. Then he became a church-planter and pastor in Bolosso. Samuel and Markos, like Tassew and hundreds of other Christians, suffered abuse, mistreatment and imprisonment for Christ.

Tassew went to school and then to Bible School to study the Word of God and to prepare for full-time service. He trained to be an evangelist and spent many years in distant provinces preaching the Gospel and planting new churches. Like so many others, he suffered beatings and imprisonment during the Derg, the communist regime that lasted for seventeen years. Tassew still bears on his body the scars that his father inflicted. They are the scars he is glad to bear for Jesus! And he thanks the Lord for the strength God gave him to choose the right Centre-pole to climb!

18

ALDABO

The Crooked Tree
ಜ❀ೊ

Do not fear, for I am with you; do not be dismayed, for I am your God. I will strengthen you and help you; I will uphold you with my righteous right hand. All who rage against you will surely be ashamed and disgraced; those who oppose you will ... perish.

Isaiah 41:10-11

Aldabo just bubbled with excitement as we neared the village. We were going to a district Bible conference, as they called their Spiritual Life Conventions. It was to be the first such gathering for a long time and everyone was excited.

Aldabo was always 'bubbling,' laughing, talking, joking, telling stories. It seemed he had a thousand fables, quips and sayings of the Wolaitta people. No wonder he was an effective evangelist; so easy to listen to and challenging, always seeking a definite response. Aldabo was one of many Wolaitta evangelists who took the Gospel of Christ to the Sidamo tribe who were the sworn enemies of the Wolaitta. They had a history over many generations of attacks and revenge attacks. Aldabo was a companion of evangelist Tassew and they spent a decade planting churches in Sidamo. Some evangelists were killed, but all considered it worth the risk to take the message of forgiveness and reconciliation through the blood of Jesus to their enemies. Aldabo and Tassew had reaped a wonderful harvest in Sidamo.

When the Sidamo Christians could manage the church affairs themselves, the Wolaitta elders recalled all the evangelists. Tassew went on to another province. Aldabo was chosen by the Christians in their district to be their leading elder. Aldabo planted a new church and served for many years as pastor, counsellor, mediator and enthusiastic visionary. He always had the heart of an evangelist, wanting to reach out to the lost, those unreached and still in darkness.

༄༅༅

The pastors and elders welcomed me warmly. In their meeting house we prayed together and shared a meal while crowds of people assembled. Aldabo was keen to show me where the meetings were to be held. It was on a nice hillside where they had erected some poles to hold up a *dass* ~ canopy made of bamboo and grass to give shade from the hot sun. I told Aldabo that it looked like the ideal place for the meetings. The gentle slope of the ground, shady trees around the edges and the leafy, grass shades over the bare places made it just right for the thousands of people beginning to gather. This convention was a special one, the first for fifteen years because the communist regime had banned such meetings. I had been the speaker at the last one, so I counted it a privilege when asked to speak at this one. So much had happened since we met here last time!

But when I reached the speakers platform, I saw that something was wrong! They had piled up clods of earth, tied it together with logs to make a platform and covered it with a bamboo mat. They planted a post with a board on top as a lectern. But, it was in the wrong place! It was not in the centre, but in front of a crooked, twisted tree. Twenty paces to the right would have been a much better place, near a shady tree. I told Aldabo that they had put the platform in the wrong place.

Aldabo just laughed! The other church leaders laughed with him. Aldabo said, "Yes, but it is the tree. The tree! Don't you remember? That is where Assefa tried to kill you. We want you to stand there again so we can praise God together for his protection and for answering prayer." Just then a group of twenty-four older ladies came and stood in front of the platform to practice the song they would sing at the meeting that day.

And I remembered.

☙☬

In missionary work for the past fifteen years I travelled all over the world, but I remembered well that day — that day at the crooked tree. Aldabo gathered all the pastors and elders of the churches in the district to organise three days of meetings. The annual convention meetings were vital for the many Christians who could not read or understand Amharic because at that time, they did not have any Scriptures translated into their Wolaitta language. They were wonderful days of fellowship, renewal and interaction.

The *Derg* ~ committee of equals was the communist government had taken over Ethiopia a year earlier. They had murdered Emperor Haile Selassie and started their style of 'cultural revolution.' They sent groups of Marxist cadres from the capital, Addis Ababa out into the towns and countryside "to eradicate all opposition to the new socialism" that promised "an end to bribery, corruption, injustice and inequality." There would be "land and food for everyone" by eliminating the rich 'exploiters,' the landowners and merchants, and by seizing their possessions and property for 'the masses.' Young Marxist revolutionaries were made Administrators and 'Enforcers' — guardians of the new regime.

The bands of cadres, led by radical 'comrades' used their power to imprison or execute anyone who dared question what they did. An exceptionally nasty and vicious Administrator called Assefa used the cadres to terrorise the Humbo district in Wolaitta. Only Ali Musa, the Administrator in Arba Minch, was considered worse! Comrade Assefa boasted of destroying all the rich, all the Westerners and all religion. During the period of Red Terror tens of thousands of Ethiopians were killed and hundreds of thousands fled from their homeland. The whole country was in turmoil. Most Western missionaries were forced to leave their stations. Their presence put the Ethiopian Christians in greater danger from accusations of "collusion with Western imperialists."

౸౦ఁ

Over a few busy, hectic weeks I gave a series of messages all over Wolaitta and other areas for church leaders. I expected a few hundred leaders in each area, but crowds turned up and the seminars turned into conventions. The teaching was especially for pastors, elders and evangelists to prepare them for the dark days ahead under the communist regime. I emphasised the faithfulness of God to be with His people in persecution, oppression, trials, suffering, hardship, sickness and imprisonment. I often used stories of the church in China, Cuba, Russia, Uganda and Congo.

It happened on the last day of the convention, on the Sunday afternoon with several thousand people present. Aldabo led the meeting and I was right in the middle of my final message when it happened. Sitting on the platform behind me, Aldabo noticed a cloud of dust rising in the distance. With his chin, he pointed it out to a pastor next to him. The pastor in turn told someone else and soon I lost the attention of the whole congregation as everyone looked at the approaching vehicle causing the dust. Then everyone started to chatter together and prepared to scatter. As it came closer we could see guns protruding out the windows of the overloaded 4WD vehicle. The vehicle was coming on the rough track from Humbo. Someone must have told the cadres there about the gathering of Christians. Now Comrade Assefa was coming himself with his cadres and some soldiers.

Aldabo jumped to his feet and shouted over the hubbub of the crowd, "Do not be afraid. Do not move! Sit down! Everyone sit down and pray! Pray! God is with us! Glorify Your Name, O Lord Jesus!" Amazingly everyone in that crowd sat down again and bowed their heads in prayer!

Everyone, that is, except a woman who jumped to her feet. Shouting out, "My sisters!" she gathered up her skirts and ran through the crowd and up the hill. More than twenty other ladies joined her in a dash for a small, grass-thatched house. I presumed they were frightened and fled. If they were afraid, they were not the only ones! When all the ladies were inside, the leader quickly pushed the bamboo door across the opening. Then she knelt on the dirt floor and put her forehead in the dust. The other ladies joined her in earnest prayer as they cried out to the Lord for deliverance.

The vehicle stopped near the gathering in a cloud of dust and about twenty soldiers and cadres jumped out; most of them armed with rifles. The cadres, in their green uniforms and red caps, armbands and scarves quickly surrounded the crowd to stop anyone leaving.

I had not seen Comrade Assefa before, but knew of his reputation for cruelty. He hated the Bible and vowed to "wipe out all religion in Wolaitta." He stomped through the people, not caring who he trod on. Two cadres followed him closely and drove the old men off the platform. Assefa pushed me off the platform towards a small tree nearby.

Aldabo tried to protest, "By what authority?"

But, Assefa stopped him, shouting, "I have the power. I am the authority. I can do anything I want." He was furious at being questioned! He stood on the platform and threw a Bible onto the ground. Assefa started a long speech with the new Derg catchphrase: "Ethiopia First," and lifted his clenched left fist in the air. He rattled off a whole string of benefits that the new Marxist, Leninist Socialism was to give "you poor, down-trodden masses."

It seemed he was unaware that the majority of the people could not understand a word he was saying, as he shouted in Amharic and did not have it translated into the Wolaitta language. For nearly half an hour he praised the Derg and condemned the Emperor and his government, the rich landlords and the Western imperialists.

Then Assefa turned to the church, "Religion is dead! Your God is dead! Your Jesus is dead! No more church! No more meetings! No Bibles! The Western Imperialists, all the missionary spies are finished too. Now we are free under the Marxist-Leninist socialist democracy. Ethiopia First."

Assefa had worked himself into a real frenzy. Sweat poured down his face; he frothed at the mouth and huge veins stood out on his neck. He looked like he would have a stroke! Was he drunk? I had not smelled alcohol. Was it drugs? He was beside himself! The cadres shouted out, "Death to the imperialists! Victory to the revolution! Down America!"

Aldabo tried to protest again, "Authority?"

Comrade Assefa rounded on him, shouting, "Authority? Authority, you say? I am the authority! I am the Derg's authority! I will destroy you and your church! God is dead! Long live Marxist Socialism!"

Some pastors and elders tried to intervene, but the cadre guards beat them back with their rifles.

The situation was getting decidedly ugly!

Aldabo shouted out to the Christians, "PRAY!" Thousands of heads bowed in prayer. It was a wonderful sight to behold!

The cadre leader pushed me back again, up against the small tree. "I will show you," he snarled, "Your God is dead!" Assefa called a soldier to him.

I said, "You only have man's authority. Jesus Christ is the Son of Almighty God. The Bible says that all authority in Heaven and on earth has been given to him."

Apparently I had just 'waved a red rag at a bull!' Aldabo said later, "Fire came from his eyes" — for Ethiopians, ultimate level of anger and loss of control was to have fire come from the eyes!

Comrade Assefa ordered the soldier, "Shoot him!" The soldier, startled, hesitated. Assefa grabbed the barrel of the soldier's rifle and pointed it at my chest. "Shoot! Kill him!" he thundered.

The strangest thing happened! The soldier could not pull the trigger! Try as he might, he could not do it. His finger seemed to be frozen stiff. He took his hand off the rifle, flexed his fingers and tried again. But, he just could not fire the rifle!

In frustration Assefa snatched the rifle from the soldier and pointed it at my head. Many pastors and church elders, the respected leaders in the community, cried out, "Stop. Stop. He is our guest, our friend."

The whole crowd jumped to their feet, shouting, "Stop. Do not harm our guest."

Against the tree, I could only say, "Jesus. Lord Jesus." I thought of Vida and our children far away.

Grinding his teeth and foaming at the mouth, Assefa had the rifle only a few centimetres from my face. But, he could not pull the trigger either! Was the rifle jammed? I don't think so. There was something wrong with his finger, too! He rubbed his fingers together and tried again. But, he still could not do it!

In absolute fury and frustration, Comrade Assefa threw the rifle on the ground and rushed through the crowd back to the vehicle. He pulled the hapless driver from behind the steering wheel and jumped into the driver's seat himself. He started the engine with a mighty roar and a huge cloud of black smoke. The soldiers and cadres came running and somehow they all managed to scramble aboard as Assefa drove off down the hill at breakneck speed.

☜☞

We all just stood there gasping, gaping, stunned and watching the dust disappear in the distance. Aldabo was the first to recover. He shouted, "Praise God. Praise God! Thank You Lord Jesus. You have all authority." He managed to get the people to sit down again and called for one of the singers to lead in a song of praise to the Lord.

Just then the door of the little house up the hill flew open and out poured the twenty-four women. (Yes, I counted them!) They were the Ladies Prayer Group of the local church who had prostrated themselves on the dusty floor before the Lord, pleading for God to deliver His people from Satan's attack. They claimed in prayer that the Lord had closed the mouths of lions for Daniel and had made a great fish spit out Jonah. God had opened prison doors for Peter and the women believed He could stop "the servants of Satan" for them, too! God can do the impossible. He is almighty and faithful and the ladies trusted Him. God honoured their faith and answered their prayers.

Now He must be praised! They were just delirious with joy and they skipped and jumped down the hill. They sang and clapped and danced before the Lord. They had not done that before, but in the thrill of what they had seen, they wanted to keep praising God. These twenty-four women reminded me of Miriam dancing before the Lord when the Israelites were delivered from their slavery in Egypt and had crossed the Red Sea.

For half an hour the thousands prayed and praised God and sang together, thanking Him for His deliverance and victory! I never did get to finish my message! I encouraged the Christians to be strong, to endure suffering, to pray, to love and help each other and to meet in small groups in their homes or in secret places. I said, "Watch and pray" and started to say farewell. I suspected it might be a long time before we could meet together again.

Just then a man at the back of the crowd called out, "Is it too late? Is it too late to believe in Jesus? I want to believe!" With his warm evangelist's heart, Aldabo seized the moment! He asked if there were any other unbelievers there, who would, right at that moment, repent of their sins and come to Jesus. Eight or nine, mainly young people, stood up to accept Christ and Aldabo led them to renounce Satan and to faith in the Redeemer.

While pastors counselled them individually, Aldabo made another appeal. He said these were dark days. He warned of trials and persecution to come. God's people must love each other — there was no time for disputes, arguments or sin. He called believers to repent and confess their sins and to be reconciled to each other. Amazingly, a hundred or more people responded. Aldabo led them in a prayer of repentance and soon there were tears of joy as peace was made with God and with people they had offended.

፨

While this was taking place, the still raging Administrator, Comrade Assefa drove like a madman over the rough tracks. We heard next day that he had ignored the pleas of the terrified soldiers for him to slow down. Going far too fast around a bend, Assefa lost control and the vehicle smashed into a tree. The driver, Comrade Assefa, was the only one killed, but several other cadres were seriously injured. That day everyone learned that God is very much alive and still *"rules in the affairs of men."*

ಬಿಂ

Now fifteen years later I told Aldabo that he had put the platform in the wrong place! How he laughed! He said, "But it is the tree! Don't you recognise it? That is the tree where Assefa and the cadres tried to kill you." Yes, it was the same tree, but much bigger now with fifteen years of growth on it — much bigger, but still crooked, still twisted and still there! It is a reminder that God is almighty, that He answers prayer and that He is always right on time!

19

ALDABO

The Man at the Funeral
ಖ❀ಆ

Do not be afraid: keep on speaking, do not be silent. For I am with you and no one is going to attack and harm you, because I have many people in this city.

Acts 18:9-10

In a different society from his own Wolaitta one, Aldabo could have made a good living as a comedian. At elders meetings or travelling along the rough tracks, he often had us rolling in laughter! He had an endless store of funny stories, fables, quips and sayings that kept people smiling, giggling or laughing outright!

In his ministry as an evangelist and pastor and later as a main elder leading a whole district of about sixty churches, he used his gift of humour to break down tensions and disputes. Aldabo's stories always had a 'point' to them that stimulated people's thinking and caused them to evaluate the worth of an argument. They often "poured oil on troubled waters." He used the African proverb, "When elephants fight, the grass gets hurt." and added, "When Christians fight, God's church gets hurt!"

One of our sayings that he particularly liked was. "Never look a gift horse in the mouth!"

Once I told him, "It is too late to shut the gate after the horse has bolted."

He thought about that for a while and said, "The wise dog barks after the hyena has passed by."

ಖಆ

When we travelled together Aldabo would share some stories of Wolaitta thieves who, for their skill and daring, were renowned all across the country. Everyone loved Aldabo, not just because he made people laugh, but also that he often laughed at himself and had others laugh with him as he did so.

At one convention meeting, I told the congregation this story: "The Lord Jesus asked his disciples to each carry a stone — 'just for Me.'"

"Each disciple found a rock and carried it behind the Master. John who loved the Lord so much, chose a huge rock and needed others to help him get it up on his shoulder, but he staggered along under its weight behind the Lord. Peter picked up a little stone, flipped it into the air, caught it and put it into his pocket. He said, 'A stone is a stone and that is good enough for me.'"

"After a while the Lord Jesus blessed the stones and turned them all into bread for lunch. John had plenty and Peter very little! Their love for the Saviour was reflected in the size of the stone they were willing to carry for Him. So, my question is, 'How large a stone are you willing to carry for Jesus?'"

A messenger came from the mission station, so I had to leave the meetings and go back to deal with a situation that had developed in my absence. When I returned the next morning, a bleary-eyed Aldabo told me that he had sat up all night reading right through the four Gospels and Acts of the Apostles and had not found the story! Apparently he was busy doing a job and had missed my introduction. Aldabo did not hear me say that it was not a true story from the Bible! We had a good laugh together about it and soon Aldabo was telling the story on himself and laughing with the people!

☙❧

Aldabo also adapted one of the 'black humour' jokes he heard from Addis Ababa about the new regime, but he was careful where he repeated it! He discreetly shared the joke with family and trusted friends. It went: "Mengistu Haile Mariam (the Chairman of the Derg, the communist government in Addis Ababa), Ali Musa (the Administrator in Arba Minch) and Assefa (the leader of the cadres in Humbo) were flying over Wolaitta in a helicopter. Mengistu took out of his pocket a $10 Birr note, (worth a week's wages at that time) threw it out of the window and said, 'I will make one poor peasant happy.'

Ali Musa then took two $5 Birr notes out of his pocket. He threw them out of the window and said, 'I will make two poor peasants happy.'

Assefa then took ten $1 Birr notes out of his pocket, threw them out of the window and said, 'I will make ten poor peasants happy.'

The helicopter pilot thought to himself, 'If all three of you threw yourselves out, you would make thirty million poor peasants happy!'"

ಐಂಡ

In Wolaitta the sayings "Everyone goes to the market" and "Everyone goes to the funerals" are literally true! No one would think of missing either! Both are important social occasions as well as times for serious business. Evangelists also found them great opportunities to proclaim the Gospel and many a believer testified of hearing the Good News in these places. But, during the seventeen years of communist rule, 1974-1991, all religious teaching was forbidden. Churches were closed, Bibles burnt and many Christian leaders imprisoned. The communist cadres who led the 'Red Terror' campaign, the 'cultural revolution' stopped all preaching and this cut right across the customs of Wolaitta society. It brought extra sorrow to grieving families. Not to farewell a Christian loved one with a huge funeral was unthinkable and not to proclaim the faith and hope the person had of eternal life, was offensive. The cadres and their spies were everywhere. They watched to see if anyone spoke about God or Heaven or eternal life. So some of the Christians had a 'public' funeral service without the usual singing and preaching, but once everyone had gone home, cadres and spies included, the Christians returned for a second 'memorial service' when the message of hope and eternal destiny was given!

༺༻

When Aldabo's ninety year old father died thousands gathered. He was a well-known, highly respected and much-loved old man. Christians, non-believers and neighbours — everyone came for the funeral. Communist officials, cadres, police and traders came in cars from the towns. Buses and trucks arrived packed with people. Some said between 15,000 to 20,000 people sat for hours in the hot sun or in any shade they could find. There were hundreds of umbrellas, with at least four people sheltering under each one!

Aldabo was determined to preach the Gospel at his father's funeral and there were plenty of people ready to take him off to prison if he did! He did not know what to do, but spent some time in prayer alone and asked the Christians to pray with him. Large groups of mourners arrived and stood before the family who sat under a marque to receive their condolences. When everyone was seated, Aldabo stood up to speak about his father. He told of his hard work and skill as a farmer, as a hunter, as a merchant and as a warrior. Everyone nodded in agreement.

Aldabo then asked, "Was my father a good man? Truly, was my father a good man?"

The whole crowd responded, "Yes, your father was a good man."

Aldabo strode back and forth before the crowd and shouted, "You say my father was a good man. You did not know my father! My father was not a good man! He was a bad man! Did you hear? My father was not a good man! He was a bad man! He was a terrible man!" The whole crowd were shocked! They stared at Aldabo. That anyone would say something like that at his own father's funeral! It was awful, unimaginable! It was just not done! It had never been done. They were all embarrassed and ashamed to hear Aldabo say it!

But Aldabo carried on his tirade, "Yes, my father was a bad man, an evil man. He was a cruel man! My father was a murderer! Do you know that? He was a thief! My father beat his wife, my mother! My father took other women. He was a terrible man! My father went across the Bilate River. He killed Sidamo men and stole their cattle. Then he came home and got drunk and beat his wife and scared his children!" Shock, horror, stunned unbelief! A wave of revulsion went through the crowd. Aldabo stopped pacing up and down. The people could not even guess what he might say next!

Aldabo had everyone listening with bated breath. He said, "Did you hear about the doctor in South Africa who took a bad, diseased heart from a man and replaced it with a good, healthy heart from a man who was killed in an accident. Yes, and he has done this several times. Is that not wonderful?"

Aldabo said, "Now let me tell you something that happened to my father that is even more wonderful than that! One day my father met a Man Who gave him a new heart! Everyone stared at Aldabo, some of them with open mouths! Aldabo continued, "Yes, one day my father received a new heart — not a fleshy one, but a spiritual one and it changed my father completely. He became a new man. With his new heart my father received a new mind, a new attitude. He had new thoughts. He was altogether different. I am not allowed to tell you the Name of the Man Who gave my father a new heart, a new life. But, that Man can do the same for you! My father was a bad man (we all are bad until we meet the Man and get a new heart) but the Man made my father a good man, a kind man. Instead of taking, he gave to others. He helped people. He loved people and became sober and hard working. Yes, my father was bad, but the Man made him different. He became a new creation. I am sad today. My father has gone from this world, but his soul has gone to live with the Man Who gave him a new heart."

As Aldabo sat down, the crowd burst into loud and long applause! None of the communist cadres or officials of the Derg government could say a word. They all quickly left in their vehicles while Aldabo led the procession to the freshly dug grave. He sang a song of praise to the Man Who makes new people by giving them a new heart.

ಶಿಂಬಿ

That night in scores of Wolaitta homes, Christian women boiled their coffee pots and roasted extra corncobs and lots of sweet potatoes. The men went around to their neighbours' houses and invited them to join their family for the evening meal. And as they sipped the hot, salty, buttered coffee, they were keen to talk about the Man who gave new hearts and changed people's lives. That night many people came to trust in Christ as their Saviour. The next morning the converts went to Aldabo's house and told him that they too, "had received a new heart from The Man!" Aldabo taught the new believers over the next few months what it meant to follow Jesus Christ — how to live and how to pray. Then one day he took them all down to the Bilate River and baptised them in the Name of The Man!

ಶಿ❀ಬಿ

20

EKASO

Prayer Warfare

⊰ ❀ ⊱

For though we live in the flesh, we are not carrying on our warfare according to the flesh and use mere human weapons. For the weapons of our warfare are not physical, but they are mighty before God for the overthrow and destruction of strongholds.

2 Corinthians 10:3-4

Ekaso's prayer life was a blessing and challenge to all of us. Those who are physically weak often seem to draw near to the Lord in a special way. Maybe God is especially attracted to the weak ones as our weakness allows His power to be fully displayed!

Ekaso believed, not only in private prayer, but also in family prayers, prayer partners, prayer triplets, united prayer, congregational prayer, prayer no matter how many or how few were present. He believed that prayer was the place where the real business of evangelism, church planting, discipleship, church growth and holiness of life, was accomplished.

When we first got to know him well, Ekaso was one of the sixteen main elders, the leaders of the Wolaitta church. He represented the churches in Fango at the eastern end of the province. He had started a church there before going out as an evangelist for many years to distant areas. He preached the Gospel among animists in Sidamo and Kafa and Muslims in Arsi. Orthodox priests, Muslim imams and pagan witchdoctors opposed him as he preached. Ekaso spent months in prison, beaten, starved and mistreated, but he kept on with his ministry. With the real heart of an evangelist, he sought to lead people to faith in Christ, in prison or out!

The pastors and elders of the churches in Fango selected Ekaso to be their representative on the Wolaitta Church Council. Like everything else he did, Ekaso put all his energy into it. Soon he was pastor of a new, growing church, mentoring younger pastors, advising and encouraging Christians, counselling the needy, supporting the suffering, comforting the sick and always, praying. He organised conventions on the mountains of Fango and guided me over the rough tracks to get there. In the hot valley of Fango's lowlands, along the Bilate River, he gathered teams of Christian men to clear tracks through the thorn trees, rocks and scrub for my 4WD Land Cruiser to get to a baptismal service or a convention.

༄༅

At the annual convention at Soddo, about 10,000 people gathered. As the afternoon session finished, Evangelist Mahae asked the church leaders for permission to present a prayer request. Mahae had brought three men from the distant Bunna tribe to the convention. These new Christians were amazed and delighted to discover that there were many other followers of *Eyesus Kiristos* ~ Jesus Christ who happily accepted them. They were not alone! Mahae introduced the Bunna believers to the congregation and asked prayer for the ministry opening up among several different tribes in the Omo River Valley. He said six new evangelists were needed immediately in the hot, arid areas to preach the Gospel of Christ. Would the people pray for God to call six men that day? Everyone said they would pray.

As Mahae sat down, Ekaso jumped up. He was leading that meeting. He led in a fervent prayer for the Lord to send six new evangelists with Mahae to the Omo Valley. As we said "Amen," Ekaso challenged men to go. Five men came forward to say they would go!

Ekaso asked, "Is there one more? Who will go?" Everyone was silent. There was no response. Then Ekaso answered his own appeal! "Then I will go!" he said. He came down from the platform and stood with the other five men!

A couple of the other elders sitting on the platform protested that he was needed in Wolaitta and in Fango. Surely he could not go? Would he give up his position and go off to the hardships of the Omo Valley?

The other elders discussed it among themselves and said, "Yes, Ekaso may go. He vowed before the Lord and before God's people that he would go. We must release him to go. God will provide another elder for Fango. We will pray for you all as you go to the ministry with Mahae."

Mahae was delighted! He only expected young men. To get an experienced evangelist like Ekaso was a bonus! The elders commissioned the six men and soon they were on their way with Mahae. Ekaso spent many years in the hot plains among the Tsemai, Erebori and Bunna people where he was used to plant several churches.

※※

Then came the Derg, the seventeen years of communist darkness! Under great persecution, all the Wolaitta churches were closed and hundreds of church leaders imprisoned. The support for the evangelists was cut off and most had to leave their isolated posts.

Ekaso came back to Fango. He prayed and encouraged the believers to be strong and resist the devil! He was distressed that the church building in his village had been closed. So Ekaso opened it up again, invited people to come early on Sunday and then preached the Gospel to them.

Spies reported him to the cadres.

Ekaso had a 'visit' from the cadres who closed the church building down again. The next Sunday Ekaso opened it up again and preached! He was warned, threatened and arrested half a dozen times, but he reopened the church each time. The spies and the cadres thought he was crazy! Eventually the spies got tired of going to report Ekaso or the cadres got tired of the long march out to Fango to close the church down again. Although many of their buildings had been destroyed or were being used by the local authorities for other purposes, Ekaso's example emboldened other Christians to meet together for prayer and fellowship in their homes or in the fields.

ಶಃಜ

On the Fango Mountains not far from his home, Ekaso had a natural platform overlooking the villages in the valley below. Public announcements shouted from there could be heard by hundreds of people who would pass the messages on to others further away. Ekaso used this platform as a pulpit to shout out the message of salvation or to give messages of encouragement to the Christians. A policeman who lived in the village below at first treated Ekaso as a madman to be pitied, then as a troublemaker who should be silenced. When Ekaso's preaching touched on bribery, corruption and injustice, the policeman reacted angrily and shouted threats up the steep hill.

After several such incidents, the policeman rose in fury at Ekaso for exposing his sin. He said he was coming to deal with Ekaso. He would stop the preaching once and for all. Neighbours urged Ekaso to desist as the policeman was cruel and vicious and was to be feared. Ekaso replied that it was the Lord who told him to preach the Gospel and provided the wonderful platform from which to do it, so he would continue to do so. He trusted God to protect him from evil men. The big policeman, still shouting out threats, came puffing up the mountain with a heavy club in his hand and with three thugs to help him kill Ekaso. As he reached the pulpit and lifted the club to strike Ekaso down, the policeman suddenly had a seizure (a stroke or a heart attack?) and collapsed. He rolled away down the slope. His accomplices lifted the policeman up, but he was dead! After that no one dared to challenge Ekaso!

ಐಂಪ

The war between Ethiopia and Eritrea up north cost hundreds of thousands of lives. The Derg conscripted more and more men and sent them to the front with very little training. Many Christian young men were taken from the High Schools and University or rounded up from the farms. Ekaso's son was killed. Mahae's son was also killed. Then Samuel's son and a thousand more. It struck the hearts of the evangelists very hard to lose their sons — the ones for whom they had great hopes in Christian service. Ekaso and his wife and their other children wept for the lost boy. Would the senseless war never end?

The war in the north went from bad to worse as the northern tribes joined the fight against the Derg and its leader Colonel Mengistu Haile Mariam. The Derg demanded more and more men for the front. An army camp had been built in the Fango valley along the Bilate River. Conscripts from the southern provinces were taken there for training. Ekaso saw the tin roofs of the dozens of barracks shining in the sun. Rumours spread about the goings on in the camp; of young men being beaten and brutalized; of many 'accidentally' killed while being trained under live fire; of a few escaping at night, but more being shot when trying to escape.

Ekaso was stirred in his spirit about the army camp that he saw every day. He felt it was evil, destroying the young men and must be resisted. He spent hours in prayer, alone or with his wife. Then he went to Soddo and brought two men to Fango to pray with him. He could not have chosen two better men to pray for victory — not against men, but against the spiritual forces of darkness that controlled them. Ekaso called two men tested in the fires of suffering; men who had been imprisoned and who knew God answers prayer. Waja was the leader of all the Wolaitta churches and Markina was the coordinator of all the Wolaitta evangelists. They were the best men to call into prayer warfare against the devil.

Ekaso took Waja and Markina to his 'pulpit' and showed them the army camp in the distance. "Let us pray for God to destroy, to completely destroy the whole camp — today!" he said. The three men prepared themselves for battle. They all called on God to show His mighty power and bring glory to His mighty Name by removing that evil thing in the valley. They prayed for the camp to be wiped out. In a day!

They prayed an 'impossible' prayer and believed the Lord would do it. Ekaso lifted his arms, raised the palms of his hands and pushed. Waja and Markina joined Ekaso in pushing with their arms and asking God to push the army camp right out of the valley. Later in the twilight, they walked to Ekaso's house, trusting God to do the impossible. The camp had been there for years. There was nothing the three prayer warriors could do, so by faith they claimed the victory and praised the Lord together.

Early next morning Ekaso led Waja and Markina and his family back to the platform and looked down into the valley. An amazing thing was taking place before their eyes. The camp was destroyed! It was disappearing! It was melting away in every direction, disappearing before their eyes! How they rejoiced and thanked God for what He had done! From that pulpit they proclaimed the glory, power and majesty of the Lord!

The Lord was answering their prayers in ways greater than even these faithful men could hope. In the north the tide had turned. The army of the Derg was capitulating and all army units were in retreat. As they headed south, the soldiers fought a delaying, rearguard action and abandoned much of their heavy equipment as they did so. The Derg ordered all soldiers to report to the capital, to defend Addis Ababa. They were to leave immediately. Overnight all the soldiers at Fango camp loaded their guns and ammunition and moved out in a long convoy of trucks. By dawn they were all gone. News of their departure quickly spread through the villages.

The people of the area had been exploited for so long because their grain and animals had been seized to feed the soldiers. They hated the army camp. Now, like a giant swarm of buzzing bees, they poured into the camp and literally tore it apart. Soon men were walking off with loads of roofing iron, timber doors and shutters on their heads. The women carried away heavy loads of wood across their backs. Some loads were taken across the Bilate River and in every other direction and soon it all just disappeared! The children collected piles of live bullets, clothes and cooking pots that were left behind in the soldiers' rush to leave. Just a few welded steel posts were left stuck in concrete slabs. In a few hours absolutely everything was gone!

The retreat of the army in the north became a rout and thousands of soldiers took their rifles and disappeared back into their home areas. The Derg, the communist government in Addis Ababa collapsed and the army surrendered. Most thought only of flight to escape the revenge of the victors. Colonel Mengistu Haile Mariam took his family and his top generals with him, plus, reportedly, 100 million US dollars, and flew off into exile in Zimbabwe with the help of his 'friend,' President Robert Mugabe!

৪০০৪

The communist era passed and freedom came back to Ethiopia; the closed churches were reopened and the destroyed ones were rebuilt, bigger than before. They found that the number of Christians had doubled, then doubled again under the oppression as the 'house churches' used 'friendship evangelism' to spread the Gospel and thousands had been won to Christ.

It was time for Ekaso to move out again. The unreached Arsi Muslims beckoned him and he spent several years preaching the Good News in Seraro district and Ajee town. He was eighty years of age when his own health and that of his wife led to their 'retirement.' For them that meant a full-time ministry of prayer and praise! They are busy at it still!

21

BEKELE

Brigands and Blessings

You will not fear the terror of night nor the pestilence that stalks in the darkness. "Because he loves Me," says the Lord, "I will rescue him; I will protect him. He will call upon Me and I will answer him; I will be with him in trouble, I will deliver him."

Psalm 91:5-6 & 14-15

It was one of those frustrating and seemingly wasted days! Just when we were so busy building too! It was a long way from our mission home at 2,590 metres (8,500 feet) altitude on top of the mountain down to the airstrip and on some previous occasions it had proved to be quite annoying. The airstrip was in the valley 1,219 metres (4,000 feet) lower down and seventeen kilometres away. Mission leaders in Addis Ababa asked me to meet a visitor from overseas who would be on the Ethiopian Air Lines flight that day. For a week I was to show him the different aspects of the ministry: medical, evangelistic, church planting and Bible teaching work. I was to take him trekking with me for a few days to some villages and then return him to the airstrip for the next flight back to Addis Ababa. I was not very keen on the idea as the aeroplane flights were often unreliable. The plane, an old Dakota DC-3, might come, but then it might not!

For two years running I hired some extra mules to accompany my own two to bring up the visiting speakers for "the Bible Conference" as we called the annual convention. Both times the flights had been cancelled without notice and I was left to prepare and deliver eight messages myself. No doubt the thousands who came for the convention were disappointed — but none as much as I was! I had to organise the meetings over the four days: erect the *dass* ~ a grass covered canopy; have workers collect lots of grass and *insett* ~ false banana leaves, for people to sleep on; have water carried from the spring and have discussions with the pastors, elders and evangelists. And then, I had to do most of the speaking!

Fortunately the elders were willing workers and capable organisers and several evangelists were competent Bible teachers. Everyone pitched in to help! The convention ran smoothly and despite the lack of visiting speakers, we experienced much blessing. Many people came to accept Christ as Saviour and some believers were reconciled to each other after disputes had broken fellowship in their churches. Some men offered themselves for service as evangelists and the believers gave cash, clothes, animals or grain and coffee beans, or made pledges to support the evangelists in their outreach with the Gospel of Christ.

The day started early! Our main worker was away visiting his family and a new worker, Bekele, was the only one available to go with me. He was willing enough, but soon showed that he knew little about saddling mules. The mules were uncooperative — but are they ever anything different? It was first light when we set out, taking the steep short-cut track straight down the mountain. This meant we had to walk most of the way to the valley floor, as the path was too steep to ride the mules. Once in the valley, we rode at a trot so that we could be at the airstrip before the arrival time of the plane at nine o'clock.

༄༅

We need not have hurried! The plane was late again. We found a bit of shade and waited for the plane to arrive.

We waited and waited! There were no radio transmitters or telephones to find out the situation. All we could do was wait — and wait! It was another hot day in the valley and the hours passed slowly. By noon we started to wonder and by two o'clock we doubted that the plane would come at all. But, we had to wait until well after four o'clock before we could be sure that the plane would not come that day, as several times it had been that late.

No plane! So, with nightfall coming on we mounted the mules and set off at a fast pace, heading for home. It was necessary to take the mules up the much longer road that trucks used during the dry season. For a few months each year, trucks brought in goods for the shops in the market place and took out the bags of coffee beans and spices. The mules had been eating grass most of the day and we watered them at the little stream near the airstrip. I was glad I had brought a torch with good batteries. It was a four-hour trip and it would be dark long before we arrived home.

ఠఁణ

For an hour we made good time up the mountain though I had to urge Bekele to keep up with me. Bekele was leading an extra mule. Our pace slowed down, as we got higher up the mountain. Bekele fell further and further behind on his mule and I stopped several times to let him catch up. We were only halfway home when the darkness set in, but the mules didn't seem to mind. They kept plodding along the very outside edge of the road, quite oblivious to the fact that if they slipped, it was a steep drop into the gully below.

We passed the rocky outcrop, the scene of many truck accidents. On my first trip up Bulki Mountain, our truck tipped over at this spot, sending a good part of the load into the valley below. The village of Mirozwala nestled in a clearing below. We could smell the smoke from their fires as women brewed coffee and prepared their late evening meal.

Bekele now lagged a long way behind. I stopped and was going to call out to him to hurry when suddenly he gave a shout of terror. Four men had rushed up the road behind him with heavy clubs in their hands. They were robbers, intent on stealing the mules. They tried to snatch the reins out of Bekele's hands. Startled, the mules jumped and kicked. A robber struck Bekele across the shoulders and he fell from the bucking mule. It made Bekele cry out all the more. He feared for his very life!

I heard Bekele's distress cry and jumped off my mule. I tied the reins to a bush and went running back to Bekele. Two robbers tried to smash Bekele's head and silence him, but they could not see well in the darkness. Bekele received lots of blows as he twisted and rolled on the ground trying to get away! "Help me! Save me! *Shiftas!* ~ Brigands!" he yelled. The other two robbers caught the mules and were trying to drag them off the road when I arrived.

Flashing my torch up and down and sideways, I shouted out at the top of my voice the old Ethiopian war cry: "WHAAA!" and charged right at the robbers! They got such a shock at all the noise I made and probably thought there were more than just me. Maybe they thought I was armed to race straight at them, screaming like a madman! The robbers just panicked, dropped their clubs and ran! The other two let go of the mules and fled, too.

By this time the whole village below had come to life and men started shouting to find out what was the matter. I shouted out, "Thieves! Brigands! Police!" I caught the mules, tied them together and lifted Bekele up. He was bruised and bleeding, but was not seriously hurt — more scared that hurt! It could have been so much worse! When I remounted my mule, I followed Bekele all the way home.

Bekele kept repeating, "You saved me. You saved my life. They were going to kill me. Thank you. Thank you." I whipped the mules on as fast as I could. The robbers might catch up with us and try again. When we arrived back at the mission station, Vida dressed Bekele's wounds, gave him some painkillers and sent him to bed. We gave him the next day off from work, but Bekele spent the whole day going about, telling and retelling the story of the robbers to the other workers and to the patients who came to the Clinic!

༺༻

After the incident with the robbers, Bekele stayed on to work with me on the buildings and to save some of his wages. Then he returned to his home in the valley and soon married a local girl that his parents chose for him. The next year he went to the Bible school and studied the Word of God. Shortly after that, at a convention he offered himself to the Lord for service as an evangelist. The church leaders appointed Bekele to distant Zala where for the next five years, he preached the Good News with great effect. Some of that time was spent in prison with many of the new believers. It was a time of great persecution and suffering, caused by the cruel Zala landowner. Despite all the opposition, the new Christians established several new village churches in the Zala area.

The church leaders reassigned Bekele to the Gofa district and he often preached in villages around the Mirozwala area. Experienced evangelists were needed out in Basketo and Bekele served the Lord there for more than twenty years. The rapidly growing movement in Basketo saw seventy churches established when thousands of people came to faith in Christ, despite much opposition and persecution.

And what about Mirozwala village? The population tripled in number and the village itself grew and doubled in area, spreading over the steep slopes. Eventually the Gospel of Christ came to that village, too. An evangelist settled there and told the Good News about Jesus, about atonement and forgiveness of sin. What about the robbers? At least one of the gang that accosted us on the road that night heard the Gospel of salvation by faith. He repented, openly confessed his sins and accepted Christ as his Saviour. We know this because he later became one of the elders of the *selot bet* ~ prayer house that was established in Mirozwala. That prayer house, now a good sized church, has more than 400 people who meet to worship God and pray together.

EPILOGUE

In 2005 evangelist Bekele came to see me at a Seminar in Basketo. What a great reunion we had! He kept telling me that I saved his life and I told him I was young and crazy! Bekele came to share in the two days of Bible teaching for the church leaders — pastors, elders, evangelists and Bible School students. The years had gone by so quickly. We talked together of those old times when he worked with us for a few months at Bulki. His wife had borne ten children, but two had died as babies. Two daughters were married, but the rest of the family were still living at home and going to school. At his present church in Basketo there are about 500 members. Praise God for His grace and keeping power through all the years!

22

TUMOLI

The Gangster
ಬ✤ಅ

Neither adulterers, nor homosexuals, nor thieves, nor extortioners will have any share in the Kingdom of God. And such were some of you. But you were washed, you were sanctified, you were justified in the Name of the Lord Jesus Christ.

1 Corinthians 6:9-11

Tumoli stood motionless in the darkness, watching his men go to work. He admired their efficiency as they quietly worked on the house. They tied the wooden door shut and stacked their bundles of dry grass against the door and along the walls. It was well after midnight and the whole village was asleep. Tumoli moved forward and as the men gathered around him, he opened the clay jar and blew on the coals that immediately started to flame. The men quickly took their lighted torches and lit the thatched roof and the piled up grass. They rushed out of the village and then stopped to watch as the flames rose higher and higher.

Then the awful screams started as the family woke up and tried to escape, the whole village woke up, people shouted, "Fire!" and ran to the house, the terrified animals tried to break their halters. It was too late! The villagers could do nothing to help or answer the last screams of the family as the roof collapsed. Soon the villagers would find the clay pot with the coals he had left behind. Then everyone would know that Tumoli had struck again!

As they hurried away through the darkness, Tumoli muttered, "Idiot! What a fool! To keep his $20 Birr, he lost everything, family, house and animals! A fool is what he was! At least the others will pay up quick." The eight members of his gang laughed with Tumoli. If any of them had any qualms about the horrible murders they had just committed, they certainly did not show it. This was not the first time they had done this, nor would it be the last.

ಬಿಲ್

Several months before, Tumoli had visited the owner of the house they had just burnt down. Politely he asked, "Is this your house?" and when the man affirmed that it was, Tumoli said, "No, it is my house now, but you can buy it from me for $20 Birr." — then about a month's wages.

The owner of the house became angry and would not pay the extortion amount demanded. Tumoli smiled and walked away saying, "I will come again and take my house." He had returned that night and collected his house!

In a few days, when things had settled down, the gang came back early in the morning with their faces covered and only their eyes showing. They extracted $20 Birr from every house in the village, taking animals if they did not have the ready cash. Tumoli then led the gang to one of their hideouts near the Omo River or into a cave on the mountain.

Tumoli had terrorised a large area of Wolaitta and surrounding districts over several years. Some people called him "*Shaitan* ~ Satan" and some "Killer" and some parents even frightened their children by saying, "Tumoli will get you!" The authorities named him as their **"NUMBER ONE: WANTED CRIMINAL"** and offered a large reward for his capture **"DEAD OR ALIVE."** But, the police could not capture him. They had a growing list of more than thirty murders and dozens of burnt homes they wanted to question Tumoli about. But still, they could not catch him!

ಬಿಲ್

I drove Vida and our friend, Melele out to speak at a Women's Bible Convention. It was on the far side of the 3,000 metre (10,000 foot) high Mount Damota in the centre of the Wolaitta district. Hundreds of women came in groups, singing as they came. They were such a happy lot! The new convention, just for women, was the highlight of the year and they came to make the most of the three days of meetings. Many of the ladies carried babies on their back and bundles of food on their heads. Others clubbed together and loaded their bundles onto donkeys. Soon twenty, then thirty donkeys were tied by their ropes, munching grass and "heehaw-heehawing" to greet each new arrival! While the ladies held three meetings a day, Evangelist Aldabo and I gathered the pastors and elders together for prayer and Bible study.

At night everybody — thousands of men, women and children — came to see the Bible pictures. Vida had sewed some sheets together to be a screen. We hung it up between a pole and the corner of a building where the people had put about thirty donkeys for the night to keep them safe from the hyenas. I ran a small projector off the battery of our 4WD vehicle. People sat on both sides of the screen. In that way thousands could see the pictures and hear the Gospel message.

First I showed filmstrips of African animal tales by the Jungle Doctor, Dr Paul White. I told the story in Amharic and Aldabo translated it into the local Wolaitta language. Then we applied the Scripture lessons from the stories.

As I showed the "Life of Jesus Christ" filmstrip, the people sat enthralled at the story of His life, His teachings, and His death and resurrection. They sucked in their breaths in excitement at the many miracles He performed. They beat their chests at the injustice of His trial and crucifixion and they wept at the cruelty of His death. But then, they clapped and shouted in triumph when He rose from the dead!

On one night nearly six thousand people gathered and there was a lot of singing and teaching of God's Word as we watched the sun go down. When it was dark I started to show the filmstrips. Then a group of men arrived and sat down on the edge of the crowd. They did not sing and they kept their heads and faces covered with their shawls. Only their eyes peeped out to see the pictures. No one knew who these men were and no one took any notice of them. It would have been quite different if they had known!

ಬಂಡ

That night, Tumoli and his gang were on their way to burn down the house of a Christian family. Some months before, the man had refused to pay the extortion money. The believer said he trusted God to protect him and his family. Now Tumoli would show him! As they walked in the darkness they heard singing in the distance. They wondered why thousands of people were gathered in the darkness. As they approached the sound, they saw a light come on as I started the film show. As the pictures of the African animals came on the screen they edged closer. Covering their faces, they sat on the edge of the crowd to watch the pictures. Other people came and soon they were surrounded.

That night, for the first time, Tumoli and his men heard the Gospel of Jesus Christ. They heard about the holiness of God, the sinfulness of man and their need to repent and to trust in Christ for forgiveness. They could freely receive God's gift of salvation. They could be forgiven. Somehow, suddenly, it all made sense to them. It was so real, so different, and so important! They sat there listening, wondering, coming under deep conviction of sin.

I showed a picture of Jesus coming into Jerusalem. Just as the picture showed Jesus sitting on the donkey, all the donkeys that were tied in the building started to bray! Their timing was perfect! A man in the crowd shouted, "They are greeting their brother!" The people exploded in laughter! They just roared! It really was so funny! The people quietened down when the donkeys did. The story went on through the trial and crucifixion of the Lord Jesus. It showed the cost the Lord paid for our redemption. Everyone was still. What a great opportunity to press the claims of Christ and urge the unbelievers to accept the Saviour!

༺༻

Just before I could make the appeal, the 'enemy' arrived! He came as a tiny little bug — a moth, a fly, a beetle or a mosquito — I don't know which — but it flew into the projector. When it landed on the hot lens, it started to go round and round. Up on the screen it looked like a long, black animal and it wrecked the film show! Someone shouted out, "It's a rat!"

Someone else shouted, "Kill it! It's a bush rat! Kill it!"

In the front row, right in front of the screen, an old man jumped up with his long walking stick in his hand. "I'll get it," he shouted and lunged at the screen. With his stick, he whacked the sheets at the top where the 'animal' seemed to be. By the time he struck it, the shadow had moved to the bottom of the screen. The man made several attempts, but missed the moving target every time!

A young man shouted, "You silly old man, you missed it!" Everyone laughed!

People from all parts of the crowd shouted advice! "Hit it! Kill it! Up there! To the right! No, the left!, Higher! Someone else hit it! Grab it with your hands! Let me try!" It was all so funny! We laughed and laughed.

Finally I came to my senses and covered the front of the projector with my hand. I pulled the filmstrip out of the projector. There was no point in trying to show more. The whole place was in an uproar! It was worse than the crowd at the weekly market. The noise of thousands of people was deafening! I blew the bug out of the projector and the 'animal' disappeared off the screen. Only the light remained. I thought the moment was lost. A great opportunity gone by!

But it wasn't lost — God has a sense of humour too! Aldabo and I stood in front of the screen in the glaring light to quieten the people and to get them to sit down again. It took us about five minutes to do so, but it was worth it! Again we told the people of God's holiness and of His grace and love — and also His hatred of sin. We told them that He would forgive those who repent and trust in His Son, Jesus Christ. I quoted Isaiah 1:18: *"Come now, let us reason together," says the Lord, "Though your sins are like scarlet, they shall be as white as snow; though they are red like crimson, they shall be as wool."*

I said, "No matter what you have done, no matter how you have sinned, God will forgive you and give you a new heart, a new life. Come to Jesus now!" And they came! First a man, than another, then three ladies, a couple, some young fellows, a family, some girls, and more men — they all came out the front to join us in the light. There were more than thirty of them. They wanted to believe in the Lord Jesus. They renounced Satan and accepted Christ "with two hands," as they say. We called for more to come to the Saviour.

Suddenly in the crowd, five men stood up and started to come to the front. It was Tumoli and four of his gang! The others disappeared into the darkness. Tumoli and his men uncovered their heads. The crowd gasped! "It is Tumoli," they whispered, "It is Tumoli and his killers! They want to believe too."

Yes, those five terrible men came up into the light. In front of everyone, those murderers, arsonists, extortioners, knelt down and wept as they confessed their sins. They renounced their old life and they trusted in Jesus, just like little children. They did this in front of people who could want revenge. Some of their relatives, no doubt, were among Tumoli's victims. But, the Christians gladly accepted them as new believers. We all rejoiced with them because as Paul tells us in 2 Corinthians 5:17: *if anyone is in Christ, he is a new creation; the old has gone, the new has come!*

It was an exciting climax to the Women's Convention!

৪০০৪

The church elders and pastors took Tumoli and his men into their room to counsel and pray with them. They talked and prayed most of the night. The next day Aldabo and a dozen church leaders accompanied Tumoli and his gang to the nearest police post.

That caused some consternation, a real panic, because they took their weapons with them. The officer was away when they marched in and laid down their rifles, a pistol and two grenades. The young constables were scared and did not know what to do. Tumoli made a full confession of his crimes. He had confessed his sins to God and to the people, but now he admitted his crimes to the authorities. The policemen, very confused, asked Tumoli why he told them.

Tumoli said, "Last night I believed in Jesus Christ as my Saviour and Lord. I am a new man now. I am not the old Tumoli. I am a brand new man and have peace with God."

The young policemen did not know what to do with Tumoli. They did not have a lock-up to put the gang in and without orders from their officer they could not leave the post and take him elsewhere. Finally they said, — and this could only happen in old Ethiopia! — "Go in peace. When we want you, we will call you to the court." So Tumoli and his gang were released into the care of the church leaders!

His conversion thoroughly transformed Tumoli. It seemed he could not get enough of God's Word. He was always going to prayer meetings and walked long distances for fellowship with other Christians. He also worked hard on his land and was always ready to help others. Tumoli was baptised with his wife when she also came to Christ. He built a *selot bet* ~ prayer house on his land near his own house and invited pastors to come and teach his friends and the neighbours that he gathered there.

Soon afterwards, widespread unrest erupted in the government schools. That led to military intervention and started the communist revolution that overthrew the government of Emperor Haile Selassie. Crowds of people then went berserk, rampaging through the towns, looting shops and burning government buildings. For a time there was total anarchy. The police post was destroyed and with it all of the records, weapons and accumulated evidence. As a result, Tumoli was never called to answer the charges that made him **"NUMBER ONE"** on the **"MOST WANTED"** list.

People who live on the slopes of Mount Damota testified that Tumoli was "changed inside and out." He truly came out of darkness into the marvellous light of Jesus Christ.

ಸಃಚ

Ten years went by before I met Tumoli again and I did not recognise him! He was so different, his face so soft. When I first met him on that dark night of the Women's Convention, his face was so hard, like chiselled granite, with the ravages of sin etched on it. He had a smell about him then, like the smell of death. Now his face was so soft that I had to reach out and touch it. To God, and to Him alone, be the glory. Tumoli certainly was changed — a new creation in Christ.

23

TONA

Spiritual Warfare
ಶಿ🌸ಲ

The prayer offered in faith... The earnest prayer of a righteous man is powerful and effective.

James 5:15-16

The weapons we fight with are not the weapons of the world. On the contrary, they have divine power to demolish strongholds.

2 Corinthians 10:4

Hardly ever before had I felt such a feeling of dark oppression and I stood still, frozen in my tracks. A shiver went up my spine, my hearts pounded and I felt very afraid. Then I saw the shadow up ahead move! Not twenty metres away, silhouetted against the sky, was a man. He held a large spear in his hand and he looked like he knew how to use it. Behind me the mule suddenly snorted and the man whirled around and raised his spear high!

ಶಿಲ

That day I wanted to stay at home. The rain had pelted down all night, gutters overflowed and the muddy mountainsides would be slippery and dangerous. The mules would be little help on much of the trail and the thought of the fourteen hour trek down to the valley near the Omo River was just too much! The river crossing might be impassable — better to stay home!

I wanted to leave at first light, but it was after seven o'clock before evangelist Setta and the three other Christians arrived to go with me. After he greeted us, Setta said, "It will be a difficult journey, but you promised to go today and Tona is expecting us tonight. He has prayed for months that this visit will challenge the darkness in the valley. Let us go."

"Why did I let myself get into this," I thought as I looked ruefully at Vida.

She said, "We will be praying for you," as she handed me the bag with sandwiches and a torch. With my four companions, I plunged into the rain and leading my mule, and started through the mud.

When the old man Tona invited me to his village to preach the Gospel, I could not refuse. His love for the Lord and his cheerful enthusiasm were always an encouragement and his earnest prayers were a challenge. Tona was the first person in his area to believe the Gospel message and turn to Christ. Now he wanted his own people to trust in Christ, but there was strong opposition.

He said, "The valley is just full of sinners!"

ಬಿಂ

Years before a travelling evangelist had led Tona to Christ and taught him how to pray to God, his Heavenly Father. Tona gathered his family and neighbours together to hear the Good News. Soon he had a small group meeting in a little grass-thatched *selot bet* ~ prayer house for prayer and worship. None of the people could read the Bible, but an evangelist came regularly to teach the Word of God and conduct reading classes for young and old.

Tona never learned to read well, but he prayed — about everything. He memorised Bible verses that were soon applied to his life and shared with others. Mostly he prayed.

Especially he prayed for the witchdoctor up on the hill. Yes, he prayed often for his friend Feltamo, the witchdoctor. Tona led groups of the new believers to witness to all the villages of the area. Slowly the number of Christians grew, but opposition soon began. The believers still faithfully shared their faith — and prayed. Tona prayed continually for Feltamo.

Feltamo lived in a grove of trees overlooking the villages in the valley. He spent most of his time in his *Shaitan bet* ~ Satan house where he mixed medicines of herbs, leaves, roots and berries. He made poisons with which he terrorised and enslaved all the people. They were so afraid of Feltamo that they brought him gifts of grain, coffee and animals to make sacrifices to appease the spirits. His divining of reasons for sickness, drought or floods usually meant innocent people were blamed for everything that went wrong. They placated the spirits with more gifts for the witchdoctor. This made Feltamo very rich.

Outside Feltamo's house, tall bamboo grew to proclaim his satanic power. The fame of his power spread and people travelled from distant tribes to consult him for potions, charms, spells, and poisons or for healing. They referred to him as "the power of Satan" and brought gifts. A stone altar around a small acacia tree near his Satan house had bowls of blood, milk and grain on it. Cotton hung on the branches of the tree and women rubbed butter onto its trunk.

Few people could withstand Feltamo's evil power and influence. And that is why he hated Tona so much!

๛ଓ

Tona and Feltamo had been the best of friends who had grown up together. Tona's decision to follow Jesus Christ had separated them, but Tona prayed fervently for his boyhood friend for years. When Feltamo heard of Tona's praying it infuriated him and threats were made against the 'new religion' and its followers. False accusations were made against the 'Jesus people' and the leaders were beaten. Tona was badly whipped and chained in prison for many months. He was left with scars that remained with him all his life. But, the believers stayed faithful to the Lord and they kept on meeting and praying.

Three times their prayer house was burnt down, but each time the Christians built a bigger one! Tona's young son was poisoned. Another son was mysteriously killed while guarding his father's cattle herd. Tona's mule had a leg broken and had to be destroyed. Several of his cattle disappeared or died suddenly and the witchdoctor's herd devoured Tona's crop of corn. It was unsafe for Tona to walk the trails alone and unarmed.

One night Tona's house was set alight and when the family inside awoke and tried to open the door to escape, they found it was tied shut on the outside. A weak spot in the wall near the cattle stalls enabled the family to escape with their lives, but they lost all their possessions.

When Tona's family sought revenge, Tona forbad them saying, "That is not the Jesus way. His way is forgiveness and love. I gave everything I have to the Lord Jesus and I will trust Him."

And, Tona kept praying — especially for Feltamo the witchdoctor.

༄༅

I knew nothing of this as I slipped and fell a dozen times on my way down the mountain. All I knew was everything had gone wrong that day! The river was flooded! Bushes and debris flowed past the crossing. Tired, covered in mud and bruised, I wondered what to do. Surely it would be better to go back!

When all of my companions arrived, I was surprised to find they were not at all discouraged. They too were muddy and bruised, but eager to go on! Setta said, "Satan is fighting hard, so there must be a great victory for Jesus ahead!"

We joined in prayer, claiming Christ's victory over Satan and all the forces of darkness — and, we prayed for a safe crossing!

Riding the mules we plunged into the dirty water. Soon the animals were swimming and we were swept more than a hundred metres downstream. I was amazed that we were not drowned, but soon we all emerged safely, laughing and rejoicing. We hurried on our way, rode, walked, ran on flat stretches, climbed hills, crossed small gullies and rocky ground and climbed the next hill. The rain cleared and the sun turned the trip into a sauna as steam rose from our clothes and the saddles.

We stopped for a quick snack and to rest the mules. The mud slowed us down and two of the mules were tired and slowed us down further. I wondered if we would have to camp out in the open. It was late afternoon and shadows started to lengthen across the valley. We decided that Setta and I should go ahead and allow our companions to follow more slowly with their tired mules. We would send Christians from Tona's village to escort them to the village. Soon we left the three of them far behind.

As we started up a long hill, Setta shouted, "This is the last hill. Over the top and then it is downhill all the way to Tona's village." At six o'clock it started to get dark. I was glad my torch was not broken in my many falls.

When I asked Setta how much further, he said, "Much more — maybe four hours." When I just groaned, he added, "Let us pray for strength" and started talking to the Lord like He was right there alongside us.

An hour later we reached the crest of the hill, but Setta's mule had gone lame! I wondered what else could go wrong! Even Setta looked discouraged as he joined me near a grove of trees. He said, "This mule needs rest so I must wait until the brothers arrive. Your mule is strong and you should go on to Tona's village."

I hesitated. What a situation! "But I am a stranger here. I don't know the road. I will probably get lost," I replied, "Perhaps it is better for both of us to wait."

Setta urged me to go on alone, "Tona is waiting and we must not let the Enemy to win. You cannot get lost — there is only one road and it leads to Tona's village. Go through the forest and down the hill. Tona will have a big fire burning outside. You go and I will pray in Jesus' Name."

෪෬

I coaxed my mule through the trees, dismounted and started to walk down the hill. The trail seemed to get better and I hurried on, dragging the mule behind me. A sliver of moon tried to shine through the clouds. Further on I stopped in my tracks — the road divided into two trails! Which way? Setta said there was only one. "Lord, guide me," I prayed silently and started on the left hand track — it seemed the main one.

But, after fifty metres I stopped and returned to the fork. It just did not seem right!

Again I prayed for guidance and started on the other path. It was so dark, so still, so quiet. Someone far away started to play a bamboo flute. My torch batteries were going flat and I was glad when the moon came through the clouds. When it disappeared again, it was so dark, black and I felt afraid. The place seemed evil! The mule did not want to follow me. The darkness was like black velvet pressing on me. I prayed for protection, for the precious blood of Christ to cover me. A wonderful peace enveloped me as I stood in the darkness. All was quiet as I waited for the moon to appear again. As it did I saw the man with the spear and the mule behind me snorted!

"Who is it?" the man shouted and came towards me with the spear raised. Quickly I turned on the weak torch, holding it at arm's length.

"Serro! Serro! ~ Peace! Peace! It is me," I said, "I am a stranger. I have lost my way. Please help me." I was happy to see the man lower the spear!

೧೦೦೩

The man shouted towards some huts among the trees. There was a babble of voices and soon people appeared with lights — bunches of grass tied in long stalks and held aloft. The whole area was soon ablaze with light.

The man with the spear was the witchdoctor Feltamo! I stepped forward with outstretched hand, "I am John's father. I came from Waka." Feltamo dropped his weapon and reluctantly shook my hand. Tribal custom demanded courtesy and kindness to strangers and travellers. The people relaxed and crowded around. Still holding the witchdoctor's hand, I said, "I got separated from my companions. I am going to Tona's village. Will you please show me the way?" I felt Feltamo stiffen and made to withdraw his hand, but I held on tightly. Their culture obligated him to grant my request.

We soon left the grove of trees with the witchdoctor leading the way and holding the light high to show the way through the large boulders scattered over the fields. One of his lads led the mule while two more came behind with more lights. We hurried and I was glad that it was downhill all the way!

It was nearly midnight when we finally approached Tona's village. A fire was burning in the clearing with about fifty men, women and a few children singing a hymn. The refrain was "We are walking in the light" and the sound echoed through the darkness. At the edge of the village Feltamo stopped and indicated that he would return home. He had done his duty! Quickly I took his arm and said, "I have an important message for you. Please come and listen to it."

As we walked together into the village and into the circle of light, the singing petered out and everyone stared at me with the witchdoctor. Old Tona stood with his mouth open — amazed. He never expected to see Feltamo in his village! I shouted the greeting, *"Serro! Serro!"*

After a moment of stunned silence, Tona leapt forward, *"Serro! Serro!"* he shouted, "Welcome to my village." He soon had some three-legged stools brought and he seated Feltamo and me near the fire. He sent boys running to bring water to wash our feet and the women hurried off to stoke up their fires and prepare coffee and roasted corn and boiled beans. Cool honey water drinks refreshed us as we talked and waited for the meal.

People soon started coming from nearby villages and even at that late hour, the crowd grew. Feltamo watched all the activity and wondered about it all. He may have felt uncomfortable in his animal skins, matted dirty hair and unwashed body among the happy, clean and helpful people. He sat next to me and listened to Bible stories and testimonies of people who had found peace and real joy in Christ, forgiveness of sin and an eternal hope. Feltamo wondered why Tona was so friendly towards him. Why was he so happy in his 'new religion?' Why had he no resentment and hatred toward him?

There was food and singing, laughter and stories. I told the story of THE GREAT WALL, one of Dr Paul White's jungle tales, the wall that was too high, too wide, too deep and too strong that nobody could get past it. I described how the different animals tried to get over, around, under and through it, but all failed. I explained how God's Son, Jesus Christ, more powerful that Satan, demons or men, came and broke down the wall that separated man from God by dying on the cross. I read from the Bible and told how people are reconciled to God and to each other in Christ.

༄༅

Instead of going home, Feltamo stayed the whole night and all the next day. He asked me many questions about the Love of God, Christ's sacrifice and atoning blood

Setta arrived with the others and their tied mules in the morning and he shared with Feltamo for a long time as he also was from a witchdoctor's family and understood the fears Feltamo had of evil spirits. Tona told Feltamo how Jesus changed his heart and gave him peace. Over the next few days we were busy with meetings and we didn't get a lot of sleep, but Tona, Setta and I spent a lot of time in prayer, especially for Feltamo.

It was nearly sunset the next day when Feltamo, the old witchdoctor, could hold out no longer. He stood up, lifted his hand high and declared, "Now I believe. I believe God's Word. Jesus Christ is stronger than Satan. I want to walk the Jesus Road. God forgive my sins! I renounce Satan and take Jesus with my two hands."

Tona started jumping up and down in joy, shouting praises to the Lord! He and Feltamo threw their arms around each other and wept together. The witchdoctor started to beg Tona for forgiveness for all the suffering he had caused him through the years since the Gospel had divided them. Tona said he forgave Feltamo long ago and had prayed for him for years to accept Christ.

What a time of rejoicing there was in the valley that night! Singing, laughter, praying went on for hours. People kept coming to see what had happened to Feltamo. Setta and I were kept busy sharing the Gospel with all the newcomers. Over the next few days, dozens of people came to faith in Christ. We travelled much slower on the way back to Waka! We stayed one night at Feltamo's house and shared the Gospel with his family and neighbours.

The powers of spiritual darkness in that valley were broken. Many people became Christians and new prayer houses were established in several villages after hundreds of converts were taught and then baptised in a river. Tona and Setta baptised Feltamo and some of his family who trusted in the Saviour.

Praise God that He answered the prayers of old man Tona who pleaded for lost souls in the valley and especially for the old witchdoctor, Feltamo!

24

BIRHANU

Special Babies
ಸಂ❀ಚ3

He found him in a desert land, in the barren and howling wilderness; He shielded him and cared for him, He kept him as the apple of his eye.

Deuteronomy 32:10

The little girl intrigued me. She was just so cute — maybe twenty months old or a little more, with shining black skin and sparkling eyes. Hanging on tightly to Evangelist Birhanu's leg, she kept calling up to him, *"Abiye ~ My Father."* The tall evangelist smiled, stopped talking to me and squatted down on his haunches. Taking the little girl in his arms, he gave her his full attention. Her smile lit up her whole face and her eyes twinkled as Birhanu talked to her for a few minutes. Then she ran off happily to play with some other small children — but not before I had taken a photo of the two of them together!

ಸಂಚ3

Birhanu stopped in the middle of his long, loping stride. He thought he heard a baby cry. He could not believe it — not our here! There were no houses anywhere near — this area was just a wilderness. Birhanu was hurrying home. Late again!

In this area, it was not wise to be out alone so late at night, but he was delayed by the folk in the village where he had spent the day. As he told them Bible stories and explained God's love and plan of salvation, some of the older men began to ask some serious questions. Their questions were, "What does it mean to believe? Do you mean all of our sins can be forgiven? How can a man walk the 'Jesus Road?' What would it mean for us if we decided to follow Jesus Christ?" Birhanu knew it was worth the delay to spell out to these men the cost of following the Saviour. It was the first time they had shown so much interest. He knew the men would think hard about it and talk together for days. Then he could visit them again and tell them more!

It was now dark and Birhanu hurried on his way. His torch batteries were flat, but there was a half moon in the sky. With his Bible bag hanging on his shoulder and his long walking stick in his hand, Birhanu was happy and thanked God for the light of the moon. In the far distance he heard the call of a hyena and nearby in the bushes the sound of the tiny *dik-dik* ~ small antelope.

ஐൽ

Then Birhanu heard the cry again. It sounded not too far away, off to the right, in the bushes. Birhanu hesitated and prayed silently for protection. It could be a trap, an ambush. The cries continued, so the evangelist cautiously approached the sound. He found a naked baby girl lying in the dust under a thorny bush. She was only a few months old. As Birhanu picked up the child and wrapped her in his thin shawl, he saw why she had been 'thrown away' — her first teeth had come through on her top gum, not on her lower one! Many of the animistic tribes in the Omo River Valley believed that when this occurred, the baby was accursed and must be killed. At dusk, as was their custom, the elders of the tribe took the baby from its mother's arms and carried it out into the wilderness. They believed the baby had to be thrown out into the bush for hyenas, lions or vultures to eat and that if this was not done, disaster would come on the whole tribe.

Long before Birhanu reached his house, the baby was asleep, warm and comfortable in his arms. Birhanu called out, "Lo, I am here."

His wife untied the rope that held the door shut and said, "You are really late tonight." Then she saw the bundle in his arms! Without another word, she took the baby to her breast and went near the fire to examine the child. With warm water she bathed the baby and soon had her suckling on her breast. Their six children crowded around her to look at the baby while Birhanu told them how he had found her abandoned out in the bush.

Birhanu's wife cuddled the baby close. She said to the children, "She is very fortunate to have survived and she is a special, precious baby. We will call her *Tuti* ~ Precious. She is your sister now and you must help me look after her." The children laughed and clapped their hands with joy! They danced around their new sister. The eyes of the two black girls, who were darker than the other children, shone and they hugged themselves with delight! They too, were thrown away as babies because of their teeth. Birhanu and his wife had also rescued them and were the only parents they knew. Those two girls were now in school, both near the top of their classes.

༄༅

Mahae and I drove along the rough, dusty road and stopped at the little town of Turmi towards the southern end of the Omo River Valley. Together we had visited evangelists serving in isolated places among half a dozen different tribal groups. We were hot and dusty and looked forward to a couple of days rest at Turmi. The town is the hub of the area with rough tracks leading off in different directions, giving access to other tribes along the Omo River: Bunna, Karo, Erebori, Tsemai, Nyangatom and Dassanech.

Turmi is a market town and central for many of the evangelists' families. The *Kale Heywet* ~ Word of Life church leaders of the whole Southwest Zone established a compound in the town for the evangelists and their families.

About fifty of the evangelists' children are cared for in dormitories at this centre so they can attend the Government Primary School in the town. Evangelists meet at Turmi each month to pray together, discuss problems, get supplies and to attend short training seminars.

Birhanu knew Evangelist Mahae well from when Mahae had worked in Gofa. When God called Birhanu to be an evangelist, he brought his wife from Gofa to join Mahae among the Bunna people. Together Birhanu and Mahae took the Gospel message out to the people and started up a work in many villages. With the first few believers, they built a small *selot bet* ~ prayer house and after some months of teaching, handed the work over to other evangelists and moved on to new areas. If there was a hard job to do, a difficult situation to face or a hardship to endure, Mahae knew that Birhanu and his wife were the ones to send! Mahae and Birhanu served the Lord together in the Omo River Valley for more than twenty years and they are the best of friends.

It was Mahae who told Birhanu about the cruel practice of throwing away babies who got their top teeth first. Mahae rescued such babies and passed them on to other evangelists and trusted Christians to adopt and bring up as their own. He found a little boy whom he called *"Desta* ~ Joy," one of several he brought up as his own family. Desta is now in Bible School, studying God's Word and training to be an evangelist. He wants to take the Gospel of Christ to his own tribe — those who threw him away as a baby! Mahae also found several babies that he took to SIM missionaries. Some mothers, whose babies were snatched by the elders, secretly told the missionaries what had happened. The missionaries then went out at night with powerful torches and rescued the abandoned babies! Many such babies were given for adoption to childless Christian couples in other tribes.

Through the years, I have been privileged to meet many of these rescued babies, some now grown, educated and in good jobs. Some are married with families of their own, but most of them are still in school. Many evangelists in the Omo River Valley have these special children in their families and bring them up for the Lord. They are the fortunate ones! Birhanu told me there are not as many babies thrown away and destroyed now. It is because many people have become Christians and they now know that 'top teeth first' babies are not accursed — they are just normal kids!

༺༻

As they proclaim the Gospel of Christ and teach Bible truths to the converts, evangelists like Birhanu and Mahae have to confront the problems of animistic cultures. There is a custom even worse than 'throwing away' babies who get their first teeth through on the top gum. If a woman gives birth to twins, all three of them are killed, the mother and the babies. Some of the tribes that live along the banks of the Omo River throw them to the crocodiles that abound in the river. There are many other cruel practices carried out on the women in pagan tribes that leave them physically and emotionally disfigured and scarred for life. Truly, as the Psalmist said:

> *the dark places of the earth are full of the habitations of cruelty.*
>
> Psalm 74:20

The evangelists do not want to change local customs and culture, except when they are evil and destructive. They face the long-held fears that cause many cruel practices — fear of evil spirits, the spirits of their ancestors, the witchdoctors and especially the fear of death. The evangelists face opposition from the powers of darkness and from evil men. Their lives are often in danger as they preach the Good News of deliverance, freedom and new life.

Like Birhanu's little Tuti, there are scores of 'thrown away' babies who were rescued and adopted by Christians who bring them up in love. Those children will one day discover how fortunate they really are. It is so sad to think of the countless other babies who were needlessly destroyed in generations past.

Birhanu and his wife will go on living for God in some needy, isolated place, giving out the Gospel of God's love and rescuing more 'precious' babies.

25

MATEWOS

Along Unfamiliar Paths
ಬ ❀ ೲ

I will lead by ways they have not known, along unfamiliar paths I will guide them and make the rough places smooth.
Isaiah 42:16

The Lord will keep you from all harm — he will watch over your life; the Lord will watch over your going out and your coming in both now and forevermore.
Psalm 121:7-8

We ought not to be surprised, but continually we are simply astonished! What amazes us is how God prepares the way for the Gospel of His grace to go to unreached tribes, to people who are lost — spiritually lost. The Lord speaks to one of His servants — maybe a missionary — or a national evangelist — usually someone in prayer, to whom He gives a burden for a certain place, people or situation. Then they respond to the promptings of the Holy Spirit and go. And, in that particular tribe, someone may have a strange, frightening dream, or a soothsayer predicts a coming change or a villager sees a kind of vision. Sometimes it is a violent storm that makes strange cloud formations in the sky that makes people afraid, or a man overhears a curious story in the marketplace. It may be a witchdoctor who foretells the arrival of a stranger with a golden book.

Then, there comes into the hearts of some in the tribal group or clan, a desire, even a burden, to be free from the darkness and the fear of death in which they have lived all their lives. Soon there is a hunger for peace that starts people talking and asking each other questions — questions to which no one can give an answer. There is a desperate longing to be free of the bondage to evil spirits and the demands of the powerful, greedy witchdoctors. Especially free from fear of the spirits of their ancestors whom they believe remain near the village to bring harm and who must be placated with gifts at wayside shrines or at sacred trees. A few folk have a kind of 'spiritual heartache.' Is there peace, freedom, hope anywhere? The Bible says, in the Gospel of Luke that:

> *the Lord Jesus Christ appointed seventy others also and sent them two by two ahead of Him to every town and place where He Himself was about to go.*
>
> Luke 10:1

ಐಗ

Evangelist Matewos had such an experience when the Lord called him to leave Wolaitta, his home area, and take the Gospel of Christ to people in spiritual darkness among the Tsara tribe. The Tsara people live in scattered groups of small villages along the Omo River. Some are in the rain forest west of Konta where years ago, Matewos narrowly survived a raid by the Bodi warriors. That raid left thousands of men, women and children dead and the whole area stripped of all the animals, grain stocks and household possessions. Matewos was not very keen to return to the north side of the Omo River. It still held many painful memories for him — but he went anyway.

A bumpy bus ride brought Matewos to the last town at the end of the road. From there he walked from one village to another, asking for directions on the way. Then there was a long walk through the bush and although he was unfamiliar with the area, he found the way to the bank of the mighty Omo River. He wondered how he would cross the river. He was glad it was the 'Dry Season' and that it had not rained for months so that the water was lower at the crossing. He would be able to simply wade across as the water in the middle of the river reached only to his armpits.

Further down the river, he would have to pay a Kwegu tribesman to row him across. The men of the small-despised Kwegu tribe were the only ones who had canoes. Matewos did not trust the canoes that were hollowed out of a tree-trunk. They seemed quite unstable to him! In the 'Rainy Season' he would have to hire a swimmer to float him across the river while he hung on to an inflated goatskin. That was even more dangerous!

On the riverbank, Matewos knelt in prayer to ask for the Lord's protection. Then he removed his outer clothes and made a bundle of them with his shoes, medicines and papers. He collected some stones and added these to the bundle. The weight would help him from being swept away by the current. He threw lots of big stones into the river near the crossing to discourage any crocodiles that were lurking nearby. It seemed clear, so holding the bundle on his head with one hand, Matewos felt for solid footing amid the rocks and mud. In his other hand, wrapped in a plastic bag, he carried his Bible.

☯☸

As he started across the river, Matewos was surprised to see a group of six men arrive at the opposite bank. They shouted a greeting to Matewos and he called back to them, "Peace!" Then all the men started throwing rocks at him! Not really at him, but into the water near him and they shouted to him to cross quickly. They had seen a large crocodile come to the surface close by the crossing place!

Matewos came dripping up the riverbank, very thankful for the safe crossing. The men chattered excitedly among themselves and pointed at the evangelist's Bible. "Is that the 'Black Book' we were told to expect? Who are you? Did you come from Wolaitta?" they asked him.

"Yes, I came from Wolaitta. My name is Matewos. This book is the true word of God," Matewos replied, "This book shows us the only true way to God. But, how did you know I was coming from Wolaitta?" The men explained that the people of their village sent them. They were on their way to find a man coming from Wolaitta with a black book. The book would give them new life.

There had been a gathering of the witchdoctors in their area of Tsara — all sixty-five of them. After their meeting, the witchdoctors announced to the people that a man would come from Wolaitta with a black book. So the men had come to the river looking for this man with the black book. They and Matewos had arrived at the Omo River at the same time — another 'divine coincidence.' Matewos dressed again and accompanied the men to their village. All the people in the village were excited and received him gladly.

೫೦ಇ

The villagers helped Matewos build a grass-thatched house for himself and they listened eagerly as he opened the Bible and explained the way of salvation. Early each morning, Matewos worked for a few hours preparing a garden and then spent the rest of the day and evening preaching the Gospel. The people had not heard about *Eyesus Kiristos* ~ Jesus Christ before — everything was so new to them. Long into the nights they sat around their fires and discussed the stories they heard during the day.

Matewos also travelled around to all the other villages in the area and shared the Good News of the Saviour. He always opened and read from his Bible to tell the story of God's love, of Christ's sacrificial death and resurrection and the free gift of salvation to all who believed. The people seemed prepared by God's Spirit as they had a hunger for God and listened carefully to the message. They asked many questions, as this new way would impact their whole way of life and bring changes to their community. This message of peace, forgiveness and new life was what they wanted. Some people soon renounced the ways of Satan and accepted Jesus as their Saviour. Then a church was formed and together they built a *selot bet* ~ prayer house for their meetings.

Matewos then had to appeal for more evangelists to come and help him. Many more people came from other villages and groups of believers were started there too. There are now five churches in the Tsara area. Matewos thinks there will soon be other churches as more people come to faith in Christ. Five of the witchdoctors have believed the message of the 'Black Book' and accepted Christ as Saviour and Lord. They burnt down their *Shaitan bet* ~ Satan houses, the places of sacrifices, along with all their magic charms, poisons, amulets and all the paraphernalia associated with the worship of the spirits. Some of the witchdoctors moved through the rain forest to distance themselves from "the Spirit that is stronger than ours."

Let us rejoice with Matewos and praise God. Once again, by His gracious Holy Spirit, He went ahead of one of His obedient servants to prepare the way into this place where *"Jesus Himself was about to go."*

26

MATEWOS

The Mediator

&❦☙

There is only one God and only one Mediator between God and men, the Man Christ Jesus.

1 Timothy 2:5

God reconciled us to Himself through Christ. God was reconciling the world to Himself in Christ. He has committed to us the ministry of reconciliation.

2 Corinthians 5:18-19

When I told Matewos that the man must have been in a hurry, he just laughed. Whoever the man was, sometime in generations past, he pioneered the trail from Konta to Tsara. At the one very high mountain, he had climbed straight up the steep slope from the bottom to the top. He made no deviations, no easy gradients, no gentle slopes and no switchbacks on the trail to make the climb any easier. Apparently those who followed him never thought to change the trail and to this day, it remains a challenging climb for even the fittest and strongest of travellers. Not many people walk that trail through the forest, but those who do always find the climb up the mountain an exhausting experience.

Tribal people in the areas surrounding the mountain call it by several different names. Some say Mount Tsara, others Mount Konta and some Mount Oma because it is near the mighty Omo River. But most just say: "the Mountain," and everyone knows what it means. Many people are afraid of the mountain and they never climb that steep track. Instead, they go several extra hours journey around to avoid it altogether. They say it is a place of darkness, of evil, the home of Satan and full of evil spirits.

Evangelist Matewos told me that he has only climbed the mountain three times and that was over several years. I remember only climbing it once. That was enough! We agreed that the mountain is steeper now than when we climbed it the first time!

ಔಶ

On his last trip over that trail, Matewos travelled alone, which is something he rarely ever does. In that remote area, it is always wise to have a companion with you. There are many dangerous, slippery places and sometimes snakes, wild animals and robbers. Matewos had accompanied a young Tsara man out to the Bible School in Konta. He was the first Tsara believer to go to study God's Word and Matewos had high hopes that this man would be the first of many who would become pastors and evangelists, the leaders of the new emerging Tsara church.

Matewos spent a few days visiting other evangelists working in the Konta area. After encouraging and praying with the families, Matewos was hurrying back to Tsara. Running late, he rushed up the mountain too fast. He found himself sweating profusely, gasping for breath and trembling all over. He just made it to the top! He felt sick, wobbly at the knees and a bit dizzy. Sitting down on a rock, he leaned against a tree to recover.

Head down, with his eyes closed, Matewos took some deep breaths and prayed silently for strength. After a little while, he said, "Amen," out loud and prepared himself to move on. Then he heard a sharp metallic click right behind him. He was suddenly wide-awake! Matewos looked up to see five gun barrels pointing right at him! *Shifta* ~ Brigands! The brigands had seen the lone traveller coming up the mountain and waited for him. They hid in the bushes while Matewos rested and then quietly surrounded him.

"Who are you?" the leader demanded gruffly, poking Matewos with his gun. "Where did you come from? And where are you going? What are you carrying?"

Matewos answered quickly, "Peace to you, friends. My name is Matewos. I have come from Konta and I'm going to Tsara. This is the treasure I'm carrying. It is God's Word." Lifting his Bible, Matewos said he was a messenger sent by God to tell everyone about God's Son, Jesus Christ. It was a message about new life, peace and joy.

"Yes, my name is Matewos, but who are you? Where do you live?" he asked. All the guns had been lowered by this time or returned to hang on the shoulders of the gang.

The leader replied, "We are no one. We are dead men. We live in the forest. We are just no one."

Matewos quickly responded, "But, you are someone. Look at you. You are young and strong. God the Creator made you and He loves you. He wants to make you new men, His own men. Trust Jesus and He will save you. Jesus will change you."

"You do not understand. We are condemned. Everyone hates us, our families, the authorities, everyone. The police hunt us all the time. They want to kill us. We are no one," the young man responded sadly.

ఠఁౘ

Years before, the young men became sick of the poverty into which they were born and in which they were forced to live. Corrupt officials demanded bribes and greedy landowners were always asking for more rent for the land. They rebelled against the system and despite the pleas of their parents; they opted for a life of crime. They left their homes and families, stole some guns and started robbing travellers and the loaded mule trains of traders. They lived in a cave deep in the forest and kept clear of the police patrols sent to capture them. The five men had become rough, tattered and grubby. They were unhappy and sick of the life they were leading, but could not do anything to change the situation. It was now too late because government officials had posted: **"WANTED DEAD OR ALIVE"** notices throughout the area. Large rewards were offered for the capture of the rebels.

An idea suddenly sprang into Matewos's mind. "There is hope. Will you let me first reconcile you to God through Jesus Christ? Then let me be your mediator and reconcile you to your families and intercede for you to the government." he pleaded. By now it was late and getting quite dark so Matewos spent the night in the forest with the young brigands. Sitting around the fire with them, Matewos explained the Gospel of Jesus Christ, the way of salvation, reconciliation with a God of justice, love, forgiveness and peace. During the night he led each member of the gang to a personal commitment to the Saviour. They each had to renounce Satan and all their sinful ways. Matewos prayed with them and taught them how to pray too.

༄༅༆

The next day Matewos took the leader and the youngest member of the gang with him. They were brothers. They led Matewos along the path to their village and from a distance, pointed out their father's house.

While the brothers stayed hidden outside the village, Matewos located their father, took him alone to a shady tree and quietly told him what had happened. The boys' father, amazed and somewhat fearful, then called his wife, other family members and relatives in the village. After an hour's discussion, they first called the village elders and then, the whole village, to consider the implications of this turn of events. Matewos acted as an advocate for the young men and in a few hours saw the atmosphere in the crowd slowly change from hostility and anger to acceptance and joy. For years, the parents had yearned for their boys, but had given up hope of ever again seeing them alive. Some people wondered how the authorities in the distant town — and the police — would react.

The village elders finally agreed to reconciliation. After all nobody had been killed. A price could be paid for damage and loss and it would be good to remove the outlaw stain from the village. Yes, it would all be good and the elders had friends to settle things with the government officials and the police. Matewos went and brought the young men into the village. They handed their guns over to the village elders and then prostrated themselves on the ground before their parents and the village leaders to ask for forgiveness.

In that generosity of spirit we have often seen among Ethiopians, but at which we never cease to marvel, forgiveness was granted, full reconciliation made and peace restored. There were a lot of tears shed and the rejoicing went on well into the night. Matewos explained the great reconciliation the Lord Jesus Christ made when He died on the cross for us, paying for all our sin and rebellion with His own precious blood.

☼☸

During the next week Matewos repeated the process with three more families in two other Tsara villages. He was busy for days sharing the Gospel of God's grace and showing how Jesus, the only true Mediator, accomplished reconciliation between a holy, righteous God and sinful man. Matewos was privileged to lead many people to faith in Christ.

Next, Matewos gathered a group of elders, men from the three villages with the fathers of the young men. They walked for two days over the mountains and through the forest to the town where the government offices were located. There it took three more days of negotiations with the officials and the police before agreement was reached. The village elders paid a large bond to the government authorities to guarantee the good behaviour of the five young men in the future. The four fathers signed a guarantee for their sons. The police wrote an official report and the **"WANTED"** notices were withdrawn. The whole group returned to Tsara with much rejoicing.

The five young men went out and cut many loads of timber and bamboo in the forest that they carried to the village. With Matewos and the new believers, they built a large *selot bet* ~ prayer house where they meet for worship and teaching. Matewos taught there several days each week. The former gang members have helped the men in a second village to do the same.

༄༅

There really is no end to this story. It will go on to eternity. The Lord Jesus is still the Great Mediator who by His love and mercy reconciles rebels to His Father. He also reconciles bitter enemies to each other. This is all because of His work of reconciliation on the cross of Calvary. Praise Him! And He has also given to us the ministry of reconciliation — we must not fail Him!

27

YOHANNIS

Singing for Jesus

ಐ✿ಬ

As the One Who called you is holy, you also be holy in all your conduct and manner of living, for it is written, "You shall be holy, for I am holy."

1 Peter 1:15-16

Chosen that you may proclaim the praises of Him Who called you out of darkness into His marvellous light.

1 Peter 2:9

When I saw the shock on Yohannis's face, the embarrassment and apprehension — the fear in his eyes, I knew exactly how he felt! The same thing happened to me as a new Christian teenager. Shy, embarrassed, scared; I stood at the back of a group of young people on a street corner as we sang Gospel hymns to share the Good News of Christ. The lady leading the group had led me to Christ and I thank God for her faithfulness. "Aunty Nell," so we called her, took us young folk out to open-air meetings. Then one day, 'out of the blue,' she said, "Dick, come to the front and tell us how Jesus saved you." I 'died a thousand deaths,' but stumbled through a brief word of testimony — the first small step to a lifetime of preaching the Gospel of Christ.

ಐಬ

Yohannis ~ John was a young Christian learning in the Bible School at Soddo. The church leaders told me he was a wonderful singer and had a good testimony for Jesus. The elders in Offa district of Wolaitta asked me to speak at their Annual Convention and to bring a singer with me. Impressed by Yohannis's keenness to serve the Lord, I asked him to come with me to lead some singing at the convention.

Yohannis used the old Wolaitta style of telling a story in song with the congregation singing an antiphonal response. The response could be, "I will follow Jesus" or "Jesus Christ is Lord" or "God can do the impossible" or "Only Jesus Christ saves from sin" or "The Lord is always with us" or some other suitable response. Each stanza was a story of God's grace, power and redemption with Bible teaching on the Christian life. The people loved it and responded enthusiastically, singing loudly so their voices echoed to villages in the distance.

On the last day of the convention, when I concluded my message and appeal, Yohannis stood up to sing again. The people had been blessed and challenged by his unique songs and style of singing as he led them in worship and praise. As Yohannis sang of Christ's love and grace, his face shone, as did the faces of the crowd; when he sang of Christ's suffering and dying on the cross for our sin, Yohannis wept and the people wept too and when he sang triumphantly of Christ's resurrection and His victory over Satan, sin and death, the congregation responded with loud praise to God.

☼☾

I suddenly asked the crowd, "Would you like Yohannis to tell you his testimony of how the Lord Jesus saved him?" As the people shouted their agreement, I pushed Yohannis forward and whispered, "God bless you. I will pray for you."

Yohannis hesitated, perspiration pouring down his face. He had gone very pale and his knees were actually shaking! I was glad he was standing behind the pulpit and the people could not see how fearful he was or how his knees shook! Yohannis gulped, took a deep breath and in a small voice — quite different from his singing voice — started to share his story. The huge crowd listened quietly as Yohannis told of his animistic family, their fear of Satan and the spirits of their ancestors whom they believed stayed near the village in trees or rocks and who must be placated with small gifts of coffee, grain or butter and in times of sickness, with the blood of a chicken or a lamb.

Yohannis described how he often led the singing and the wailing at heathen funerals, the wild pagan dances and the drinking and debauchery that followed. He had no time for the 'Jesus people' who tried to tell him of real life, eternal life. The believers were from a village half-an-hours walk from his house. He met the pastor of that group who came to the funerals to witness for Jesus Christ. Yohannis was too busy, too satisfied with his wild lifestyle and too happy with his new, young bride, Birhanesh.

ಬಿಂ

But then one day Yohannis became violently ill — some disease that killed many others in the area. He laid on his mat for days wasting away, so sick, weak, helpless, while fever and pain racked his body. Unable to eat or drink, he became delirious, and then fell into a coma. His father was called to see his dying son. Birhanesh was afraid and did not know what to do. Relatives prepared for his funeral.

Yohannis was hallucinating. He remembered racing over the plains on his horse with spear in hand, chasing wild pigs or hunting deer. He saw again the awful pagan dances, felt the chill and fear of death, the hopelessness for the future, the darkness. Wild dreams, pain, terrible headaches, sweats and chills swept over him, as he grew weaker, thinner, dying. He heard Birhanesh crying, then starting the 'death wail.'

Yohannis's voice grew stronger as he said, "I knew I was dying and going out into the darkness and was not prepared — I was lost for ever. My father was standing near my mat weeping with my wife. I had strange thoughts.

Suddenly in a vision, I saw two men come. They grabbed my arms and seemed to pull me away through the air. Then a tall Shining Man appeared and He stopped the men who were pulling me away. He asked me, 'Where are you going?'

I had to reply, 'I do not know — it is dark.'

Then He said to me, 'Don't you know where you are going? You will be lost, in darkness, if you don't believe in Jesus. Will you accept Jesus and serve Him?'

And I said, 'Yes, I believe — I will never go back.'

The Shining Man ordered the two men who were carrying me, 'Take him back.'

༄༅

I woke on my mat to find my father and my wife wailing as only heathens do. I asked them, 'Why do you cry and wail?'

They were amazed that I spoke and my astonished father said, 'Because you died and left us.'

I said, 'But I am alive! I am going to live. I am a new man. Call the 'Jesus people' and their teacher. I want to be a Christian.' The pastor of the church came with the Christians and prayed for me. I renounced Satan and all my old life of sin and I became a child of God. He forgave me and healed me and in a few days I was well and strong again. I prayed with the believers in the *selot bet* ~ prayer house.

My wife believed too! We were baptised together. We learned to read and we read God's Word every day. I went to the Bible School in Soddo and for two years have been blessed as I have learned of Jesus and the grace of God. I thank the Lord for His mercy and I want to serve Him. Please pray for me."

Yohannis sat down next to me. His knees were still shaking. Perspiration soaked his shirt as he gasped for air. I hugged his shoulders and said again, "God bless you." The whole congregation called out loudly that they would pray for him.

☙☙

After that frightening experience, Yohannis often travelled with me to special meetings, conventions and baptismal services. The Wolaitta people loved his singing and he was often joined by other singers like Bergenae, but more and more, Yohannis was also asked to preach. It was soon evident that the Lord had given Yohannis a gift of evangelism and he was used to lead many people to faith in Christ. He also had a wonderful way of teaching Biblical truths that enabled people to remember and live changed lives. He emphasised that literate young people should, every day, read and study the Bible for themselves and also to read it to the older believers who could not read at all. Yohannis was called to preach the Gospel of Christ at meetings all over Wolaitta and at conventions in other provinces.

Young people especially, responded to Yohannis' messages and he started a special weekly meeting for students in Soddo. Soon hundreds came regularly and every week many accepted the Lord Jesus as their Saviour. Choirs of young Christians were formed for the new converts and this added to the appeal of the youth meetings. Yohannis spent hours in prayer and Bible study preparing for the meetings.

☙☙

Yohannis did not know it at the time, but these special meetings for young people were preparing them to face the dangers and troubles ahead — the persecution and suffering they would endure under the communist regime, the Derg. Yohannis led teams of young Christians to other areas around Wolaitta where hundreds of people turned to Christ.

Later, when gangs of communist cadres rounded up the whole population into indoctrination classes to learn Marxist-

Leninist ideology, the young people stood with the pastors and elders to resist the atheistic teachings and reject all that was contrary to the Word of God. When all the churches were closed, the Bibles confiscated and Christian meetings forbidden, Yohannis and hundreds of young Christians were imprisoned along with the pastors and church elders.

Yohannis and old, saintly Wandaro, who was one of the first Wolaitta men to believe and be baptised, were asked to conduct a wedding for a young Christian couple in Soddo town. Yohannis was to conduct the ceremony and Wandaro was to give the couple 'advice' and to pray God's blessing on the new Christian family. Armed communist cadres arrived in the middle of the proceedings and arrested Yohannis, Wandaro and the bride and groom. The whole wedding party were imprisoned and they finished the ceremony in the gaol!

When released, Yohannis travelled everywhere to encourage Christians in their homes and in secret meeting places. At the same time he continued his own education and this led him to the capital, Addis Ababa, where he had more opportunities to teach and preach. Yohannis was led to *Debre Zeit* ~ Mount of Olives, a town 50 kilometres south of Addis Ababa where he led a new church that included many well-educated people and several officers from the nearby Ethiopian Air Force base.

ఠఠ

When the communist regime collapsed in 1991 after seventeen years of oppressive rule, Yohannis was called to join the leaders of the *Kale Heywet* ~ Word of Life churches in Addis Ababa to have, on their behalf, a ministry of evangelism and teaching to all parts of Ethiopia. A decade of fruitful service had Yohannis preaching, teaching, studying, caring for his own family and their needs for schooling and counselling — also spending much time in prayer. It was a difficult time, physically, mentally, emotionally and spiritually, but Yohannis proved the faithfulness and strength of the Lord. Often he was called back to speak at conventions in Wolaitta and in the surrounding areas.

Although his visits back to Wolaitta were often months apart, Yohannis became more and more concerned for the rapidly increasing number of Christians in the churches there. With new freedoms, good harvests and a better economy, people had money to spend — and they spent it on possessions. Many built big, tin-roofed houses for themselves and many large congregations built huge church buildings, sometimes in competition with others, while at the same time, support dropped off for the evangelists who went out to the distant, unreached tribes. Some evangelists were recalled, many believers were unhappy and lost confidence in some of the chosen leaders. It seemed the *"first love"* of many was lost in a desire for things, for entertainment or for education. Many parents said they lost their children when they went into the growing towns to the high schools where they got wrapped up in worldly pursuits and sports programs and drifted away from God.

Yohannis knew there was nothing wrong with having a nice house, possessions and getting a good education — he had them and wanted them for his family. Not having the right priorities was the problem. Not putting the Lord first was the problem. Neglect of God's Word, prayer and Christian fellowship was the problem. That led to a cold heart, doubts, miserliness and sin. Yohannis emphasised these things in his messages and many responded, repented and returned to worship and service for the Lord with renewed zeal and generosity.

But, there were some others who sought only to get authority, position and power. They opposed the spiritual, elected leaders and started rumours and made false accusations. These disagreements and disunity erupted into disputes and divisions in the churches. He grieved over Wolaitta especially as some men gained authority by worldly, evil means, while good, spiritual leaders were pushed aside.

The turmoil grew when sects, cults and false teachers who styled themselves: "Prophets," went out from Addis Ababa into the 'church areas' of Ethiopia. They taught all kinds of false doctrines: 'Jesus Only,' 'Prosperity Theology' with all manner of unscriptural excesses and queer visions and dreams.

Yohannis found these errors spread easily because many of the church pastors and elders had only basic education and did not have much training in God's Word and therefore, were unable to respond to the claims and promises of the false teachers. Yohannis knew the greatest need was to teach Bible truths to church leaders and have them memorize the Scriptures.

With his nation-wide ministry, working out from Addis Ababa, and with his family at vital stages of their education, most people expected Yohannis to remain there in his leadership role. It was a surprise to many when Yohannis informed them that God had called him to return to Wolaitta and teach God's Word there. Some were shocked and some reproached him, but, at great loss to himself and to his family, Yohannis obeyed God's leading. Now he is calling a new generation of young people in Wolaitta to put the Word of God first and to live holy lives separated for God's service. He is training them to share the "Old, Old Story of Jesus and His Love" wherever the Lord leads them.

ଃଓଷ

God chose Jesse's son, who made music as he herded sheep, made him *"a man after His own heart,"* the sweet Psalmist of Israel and mighty King David.

Christ called a rough fisherman, Simon, to follow Him; moulded his impetuosity, disciplined his boasting, fear and cowardice in denial; then restored him, filled him with the Holy Spirit, to be Peter, a rock, a preacher of repentance and redemption.

Jesus took the firebrand brother of James, drew him extra close and made him John the 'Apostle of Love' to write the Gospel of John, three Epistles and the Revelation of Jesus Christ.

Christ stopped the zealous Pharisee Saul in his tracks with a blinding light and a questioning voice from Heaven that said, *"I am Jesus Who you are persecuting."* He swept away his soul-deadening religion of laws and the man-made rules of hypocritical self-righteousness, then transformed him into Paul the Apostle, with a holy zeal that spread the Gospel across Asia to Europe and gave us the deep doctrinal epistles of transformed life — eternal life by faith in Christ, our perfect Sacrifice and Ransom.

And the Lord took a shy country lad with many untapped natural gifts, but who was bound in the fear and darkness of his animistic family and with a question in a vision, turned his heart to faith and love and prayer and fellowship and a hunger for the Scriptures. He gave the young man a new name *Yohannis* ~ Gracious Gift of God, and made him an evangelist to win thousands of Ethiopians to the Saviour and to teach a new generation the holiness of God and His command:

You be holy for I am holy.

Leviticus 11:44

28

BELAYNESH

A Mother to Me Also
ುಃತಿ

I commend to you our sister, a servant of the church for she has been a great help to me. ... My fellow worker in Christ Jesus risked her life for me. Those women work so hard in the Lord. ... Greet his mother who has been a mother to me, too.

Romans 16:1-3 & 12-13

I know the names of more than 200 Ethiopian evangelists who served the Lord in the Omo River Valley through the years, but when I try to name their wives, I know only seven. The reason for this is that, in many tribes in the Omo Valley, it is impolite, rude and sometimes, even evil to ask the name of a man's wife. If I know the name of their eldest child, I call them, for instance, *"Ye-Yohannes Inat* ~ Mother of John," for that is polite, or *"Imete* ~ Mistress," for that is respectful. But, mostly I call them *"Ihite* ~ my Sister," for they are my sisters in Christ whom I respect, love and honour as true heroines of the faith. The next two women I have written about are good representatives of them all.

ುಃತಿ

Belaynesh, a young wife, nursing a baby just few months old, gathered up their few clothes and some 'food for the road.' She farewelled her parents and siblings, friends and neighbours and tied her possessions on her back. She put her baby on top of the load and then picked up the kettle, cooking pot and water bottle. She turned and followed her evangelist husband Mahae through the bush. She checked that Mahae had some salt and spices in the load he carried on his head. Salt was always an acceptable commodity to trade in the markets for food supplies.

What a major change this was in Belaynesh's life, leaving all the familiar people, places and things she had known all her life and to go off into the unknown. The church elders promised to pray for them and said they would try and send them some money or some grain after the next harvest. Some friends gave them a few coins that would last them for a month or two. There was no salary in those days — no promised support. They went in faith, trusting God alone to provide their needs. They expected to work hard, to establish themselves in the new community and to win people to Jesus Christ. To Belaynesh and Mahae, money and possessions were not a consideration — they never expected to be rich!

It took five long days walking through the hot valleys, pushing aside the tall grass and going up and down the ravines. They waded across deep rivers, climbed over the rocks, went up the mountains and down again, stopping every couple of hours to feed the baby. It took courage to travel the dangerous tracks where there were lions, leopards, hyenas and poisonous snakes. There were also *shiftas* ~ brigands or robbers — who preyed on travellers, especially the small, unarmed groups like theirs.

Belaynesh needed as much strength and commitment as her husband Mahae to go and live among people of another tribe who had a difficult language and different customs — a different culture altogether. For Jesus' sake, she would endure the isolation, hardships, loneliness, heartaches and disappointments.

☼☙

When Mahae rented land in Baga village, Belaynesh helped him build their house, cutting vines in the forest to tie the roof and walls together. With a sickle she cut the long grass and made bundles to throw up to Mahae as he thatched over the bamboo and eucalyptus poles of the roof. Together they dug the ground for a garden — it was hard work, but essential if they were to survive.

Belaynesh carried water from a nearby spring and made friends with the other women she met there. With them she went into the bush for firewood and learned the way to the weekly market. The hard work and the busyness of life helped keep away the thoughts of distant family, but sometimes in the darkness of the night, Belaynesh longed for the familiar ways. After a few months, however, the local activities became the familiar — this was now home.

Hospitality was a vital part of life in the new area, as in her own. Belaynesh boiled the big, clay coffee pot; added salt and butter to the strong brew and invited her neighbours in to drink it with them. As they sipped the coffee with their new friends, Belaynesh and Mahae talked about Jesus; how He changed their lives, took away their fears and gave them peace and hope. They shared the roasted grain and the boiled sweet potatoes that made up most of their diet. While Mahae made friends — how easily he made them! — by joining working bees to build a new house for a neighbour, to chop down a large tree or to plough the fields, Belaynesh traded for grain in the market or spun raw cotton to weave cloth. Belaynesh started literacy classes and taught the village children to read.

When she or Mahae or the baby became sick with malaria, dysentery or fever, there was no medical help locally, but they tried to find medicine from traders in Bulki town. Sometimes it was good medicine and worked and sometimes it didn't.

The years passed. Belaynesh was pregnant with her other babies, there were no doctors or midwives to attend her, but the neighbouring women helped as best they could. When one of her babies died, Belaynesh found it hard to control her grief as she and Mahae buried their child and tried to understand why. When they did not wail and cut themselves like the pagan people around them, but told of the love and comfort they received from their Heavenly Father, it made the local people even more curious about the 'new teaching.' They started to ask questions about the 'Jesus Road.'

Then some people left their old ways, renounced Satan and accepted Jesus Christ as their Saviour. The men worked with Mahae to build a small *selot bet* ~ prayer house with bamboo walls and a grass roof while Belaynesh and the other women made the meals, cut the grass and carried the water. When the prayer house was finished, Belaynesh made a slurry of cow manure and water to plaster over the mud walls and all over the dirt floor to keep down the dust and control the fleas. They called the smelly stuff "Gofa cement!"

৪০০৪

But soon opposition and persecution started and Mahae was arrested. Belaynesh had to carry food to the prison two hours walk away for her husband and the new believers imprisoned with him. This happened many times over the years and it was difficult for Belaynesh to care for the children and try and help the fearful believers. The persecutors made threats against her and the children. Belaynesh spent much time in prayer for safety and for their needs. The danger was very real from evil men who also had some influence with the authorities.

Some other evangelists' wives were beaten and one was killed. Belaynesh gathered the believing women for 'coffee' and they comforted each other, shared some of the Lord's promises and prayed together. The prayer house was burnt down, but months later, when the prisoners were released, she and Mahae decided that God must want them to build a bigger prayer house. So they did! Their faith was rewarded when many people responded to the Gospel, were baptised and joined the church.

༄༅

When Mahae was moved to other areas and eventually to the lowlands of the Omo River Valley among the Bunna tribe, Belaynesh bravely faced a completely new environment, cruel practices and danger every day. Bunna warriors killed two of their companions and Mahae narrowly escaped attempts on his life. Some of their children had to be left behind in Wolaitta so they could continue their schooling. They stayed with Mahae's sister Meskele who cared for them along with several orphans she had adopted.

Eventually the trying heat and constant bouts of malaria seriously affected Belaynesh's health and she had to return to Wolaitta with the children. The teenagers went on to High School. Her eldest son Matewos, the baby she had first carried on her back to Gofa, was conscripted into the army. He was sent to the war front in the north and he was killed there. This was a bitter blow to Belaynesh and it took her a long time to recover from the grief, but after, she was able to comfort many other mothers who also lost their sons in that senseless war.

Mahae continued on alone in the Omo River Valley, even after all the SIM missionaries were removed. The evangelists were left without medical help, transport or means of getting their allowances when the communist government took over the mission stations. While Mahae spent days and sometimes weeks walking back and forth to Wolaitta for supplies, Belaynesh urged the Christians in Wolaitta to keep praying and supporting the evangelists. Those years were very difficult for Mahae and for Belaynesh, too.

Belaynesh still supports and encourages Mahae. He has moved on again to the Borana tribe where he established several new churches and handed them over to other evangelists. His times of trekking and preaching in Borana get shorter and shorter as his health and strength deteriorate. Mahae says that it is only Belaynesh's prayers that give him the strength to keep going. Belaynesh and Mahae have 'kept going' together for more than sixty years. They have seen and enjoy their great grandchildren.

Salute Belaynesh, a true heroine of the faith!

28

REBEKA

Three Requests
ಏ❀ಣ

Wives, let your beauty be the hidden person of the heart, the unfading charm of a gentle and peaceful spirit which is very precious in the sight of God.

1 Peter 3:4

About forty-five years after Belaynesh first went from Kucha with Mahae to preach the Gospel in Gofa, another young woman faced the same decision in Zala. Rebeka had married Abel who wanted to be an evangelist as his father Gendalo had been before him. One of the first Gofa evangelists, Gendalo knew Mahae and Belaynesh well and, like them, had endured suffering, persecution and imprisonment for the Gospel.

Rebeka and Abel grew up together in Zala where Gendalo pastored a large church and she encouraged Abel when he went to Bible School for training. Rebeka was very supportive and ready to accompany Abel when the Gofa church leaders commissioned them and sent them to the Hamar tribe. They travelled with Birhanu, another Gofa evangelist who was working in that area with Mahae.

Rebeka had an easier journey than Belaynesh had all those years before! She and Abel only had to walk for a day, and then go by bus and on a truck for three days, before walking another day to Shonko, a small village among the Hamar people. Mahae and Birhanu had made the initial contact in Shonko, secured land and built a house and *selot bet* ~ prayer house there. Rebeka and Abel took their two small children with them. Evangelist Semayat and his wife joined them there and they had wonderful times of fellowship together. In that isolated place it was good for the two young couples to be able to support each other. A year later Rebeka had their third baby at Shonko. They thanked the Lord for this little one and also for the children in the area who were keen to learn. Rebeka loved to teach the village children along with her own little ones. Some young people and adults were showing interest in the 'new teaching,' the Gospel of the Lord Jesus Christ. Rebeka also found the mothers of the children friendly, but worried about all the wild-looking warriors who carried weapons, painted their bodies and came and went through the village.

For some months there were rumours of war, raiding parties and killings. The police post was far away and Rebeka prayed with Abel for protection and wisdom. They heard of threats being made against all 'outsiders' in the Omo River Valley. But, nothing happened and the work continued every day with the men preaching in the villages and learning the Hamar language and the women using hospitality evangelism with coffee and roasted grain.

ଏଠା

Abel had to travel to the KHC Evangelists Centre at Turmi for supplies and for the monthly meeting of the evangelists. Usually both evangelists would go, but because of some tension in the area and some wild rumours, it was decided that Abel would go alone and Semayat stay to look after the families. Abel prepared for several days away by gathering some loads of wood near the house so Rebeka would not have to go to collect it before he returned. It was late in the afternoon when he went to get the final bundle.

A hundred metres from his house Abel paused and stood on a flat rock to look across the vast Omo Valley as a glorious sunset lit up the western sky. Rebeka heard Abel call out a greeting to someone, and then give another cry as a rifle shot rang out. There was another sound of a Hamar man shouting. Semayat came out of his house with a weapon in his hand. Rebeka came outside too. They saw the flashing knife and blood spurting, Abel's mutilated body on the rock, the Hamar warrior fleeing with his gun and knife.

Abel was dead, killed by one of the people he came to help. Another martyr for Christ, he joined a score of other evangelists who laid down their lives for the Gospel. The horror of the scene overwhelmed Rebeka as the neighbours came running. All the warriors disappeared from the village — better to flee than to be found near when the police arrived — you might be blamed. Old men helped carry Abel's body into the house. The crying children were taken to Semayat's house. Numb with shock, Rebeka sat by her husband's body. Semayat was also in shock, almost incoherent, but still brave enough to run through the darkness to the next nearest evangelist. With another man he ran for hours to the SIM station at Alduba. The missionary sent a radio message to other mission stations asking for prayer and then drove thirty kilometres further on to the police post. He returned with armed soldiers and Semayat went with them and directed them through the bush to Shonko.

Rebeka sat motionless for hours, hurting, not able to comprehend, her heart crying out to God. A small litter was made; Abel's body was washed, wrapped in a white cloth and placed on the litter. Rebeka still sat there. Vehicles arrived through the bush; Rebeka heard the many police questions, but she could not answer them. The missionary tried to comfort her. At last Rebeka and the children were taken away, as were Semayat and his wife and family.

The police hunted for the murderer, but it was weeks before he was found. The police told the old men of the village that no one must go near the houses. The men said they would guard the houses. The shocked evangelists buried

Abel in the little cemetery at Alduba where other believers are buried. Stunned, still in deep shock, Rebeka stood with her children. Other evangelists and their wives gathered to comfort Rebeka and to share the Gospel of hope beyond the grave. They rededicated themselves to Christ to spread the Gospel through the Omo River Valley.

Through many hands, a message was sent to Zala. Abel's father Gendalo arrived. He visited Abel's grave, noticed all the flowers, placed some extra stones around the grave, read his son's name on the wooden cross, wept for his son and prayed. Then he took Rebeka and her three children and headed back to Zala, going as far as Sawla by vehicle. Rebeka was now his responsibility, for when she married Abel; she became forever, part of Gendalo's family.

ಬಿಌ

It was already dark when I drove unannounced into Sawla. Mahae and I had been teaching the Bible to pastors and elders in Basketo and Mallo. We were now on our way to visit and encourage evangelists among the Bunna, Hamar, Tsemai and Bodi tribes. At the Sawla church office, the church leaders welcomed us warmly, gave us foam mattresses to sleep on and provided a wonderful meal. As we ate, the church leaders asked if they could gather some of the Christians to have a meeting and if I would give the message. We readily agreed. Then they told us the sad news about Abel. Mahae and I were shocked and just looked at each other. We had planned to go to Shonko the following week!

By nine o'clock the large, tin-roofed Sawla church was jammed with people, some with standing room only. Hundreds more outside tried to get a view into the building. They blocked all the doorways and windows and inside — it was just stifling! More than 1,000 people listened quietly as I shared something of the grace and goodness of God and the love of Jesus Christ. There was a wonderful response, but now, I don't remember much about the message, the singing or the praise and worship.

What I do remember quite vividly is what followed the last song! Abel's father Gendalo rose to his feet and asked for prayer. That day he had returned from his son's grave. He described in vivid detail how Abel died for Christ. He asked us to pray that the police would find his son's murderer and that the killer would hear the Gospel of Christ, repent of his sin and accept Jesus as his Saviour. I was just amazed at the strength and the sustaining grace of God for Gendalo in light of his son's death. We all assured Gendalo that we would pray that prayer.

Then Rebeka rose and stood on the platform and she too, asked for prayer. She held her ten months old baby in her arms, as he was not well. The other two children hung onto her skirt. Rebeka said she had three requests: one, that God would give her the strength and grace to bring her children up for the Lord; two, that Abel's killer would be caught and imprisoned so that he might hear the Gospel and come to faith in Christ and three, that God would call someone else to Shonko village to take Abel's place as an evangelist.

Just as Rebeka finished her requests, her baby was suddenly and violently sick, throwing up over Rebeka and all over the platform. What a scramble of men to get out of the spray! Rebeka calmly knelt and started to wipe up the mess with her own thin shawl, but soon other women took over. They helped Rebeka and the children into a hut behind the church. After prayer, the crowd scattered off into the darkness to their homes. They would soon forget my message that night, but I know they would not as quickly forget Rebeka's prayer requests! Later I was able to pray with Rebeka and give her some medicine for the baby and a gift to help her with her and the children's needs.

꙳❀꙳

EPILOGUE

Last year, 2005, I again met the young widow. Rebeka moved from Zala back to Sawla to make a new life for herself and the children. One morning I went to her neat little house to pray with the family and to pass on a gift for which she was most grateful. The Zala church and Abel's family help her and she trades in the market for food and clothes. She prepares food for her family, pays the school fees and buys the books. The older children were in Grade 1 and Grade 2 while the youngest was in kindergarten. Rebeka was learning in Grade 4 herself. She also had a fruitful ministry to women in the town.

Back in Shonko two evangelists are reaping a harvest of souls. More than fifty people have been baptised and they have built a bigger church. All the village children are in the school they started. The children are reading the newly translated Scriptures in their own language. And yes, Abel's murderer was captured. He was sentenced to "eighteen years hard labour" and is in the prison at Jinka. I do not know the end of that story, but I heard that a couple of Christians are also in gaol at Jinka. The Lord works in different and mysterious ways and we know He answers prayer. Rebeka's prayer requests are being answered — in her family in Sawla town, in Shonko village and in Jinka gaol!

Salute another true heroine of the faith!

A FINAL WORD
Living Sacrifices
ಬ❀ೞ

I beseech you therefore, brethren, by the mercies of God, that you present your bodies a living sacrifice, holy, acceptable to God, which is your reasonable service. And do not be conformed to this world, but be transformed by the renewing of your mind, that you may prove what is that good and acceptable and perfect will of God.

Romans 12:1-2

These stories of spiritual warriors — heroes of faith and the real 'front-line' missionaries — are some of the Ethiopian evangelists who opened up vast valleys, new villages and unreached language groups of people to the Gospel of Christ. They challenge us to faithful prayer and total commitment. Often living on small allowances from their home churches, they crossed swollen rivers, climbed steep mountains and trekked long distances over the plains to spread the good news that they had found for themselves: new life in *Eyesus Kiristos* ~ Jesus Christ.

Of more than 250 evangelists we knew, that we shared the trail with, with whom we laboured and laughed and talked and prayed, most are still busy for the Lord. Some died of unknown fevers in isolated huts, some died in prison chains, some were martyred — *"of whom the world is not worthy"* — losing their lives to fierce warriors whom they longed to win for Jesus. Only the Lord knows the full story of the hardships, pain, suffering and sorrows so many of these men went through in their service *"as good soldiers of Jesus Christ."* At the command of Christ, they went forth as *"lambs among wolves,"* putting their lives on the line.

Some may wonder why I did not write 'our story' or the stories of missionary colleagues we love and respect: why not about bamboo houses with grass roofs, mud walls and cow-lick floors; of hot, spicy food; salty, buttery coffee and questionable honey-water drinks; of snakes and scorpions, fleas and bed-bugs, jiggers and lice; being lost in the bush without water or food or hope; being bogged for days in bottomless, black 'gumbo mud;' pestered by flies, tsetse flies and a million malarial mosquitoes; being laughed at, mocked, misunderstood, despised, abused, cheated, threatened, sick, lonely, afraid; of persecution and oppression; of the tears and disappointments; of the heartache of separation from our children; of broken vehicles far from help on unused bush tracks; of stubborn mules, pouring rain, flooded rives and endless mud, of scorching temperatures in the valleys and bitter winds on the mountain peaks.

Or, what about the thrill of leading a witchdoctor to Christ; seeing a family converted; preaching to a congregation of thousands and twenty, fifty or more people responding to the invitation to accept Jesus as Saviour; new churches established; Bible Schools opened; watching up to 3,000 new converts being baptised in a muddy stream; sharing worship and communion with converted spirit-worshippers, now *"new creations in Christ Jesus!"*

Or perhaps, remembering the joys of service, the sense of Christ's presence and provision, His guidance and protection; praising God for victories He won, souls He saved, the Church He established, situations He controlled, dangers He delivered from; times of distress, illness and weakness when He displayed His power and the times we heard Jesus say again, *"Lo, I am with you always."*

No!

Instead, I want the Lord to use the example of these Ethiopian Warriors to challenge you to: *"offer your bodies as a living sacrifice, holy and pleasing to God."* I want you to offer yourselves for Him to use; everything you are and everything you have; that lost tribes, that souls in spiritual darkness may hear of Jesus and His love and power to save.

I still see her now: an old woman — almost naked with a flimsy goatskin skirt — sitting on the dusty ground. Her lump of clay in one hand that she shaped into a round bowl, listening intently, for the very first time, to the Gospel of God's love. She, a slave all her life; captured as a small child from another tribe; hearing of deliverance, freedom and redemption from sin, but constantly asking, "But is it true? Is it true?"

Evangelist Mahae and I finally approaching her on our knees — to show respect and kneeling beside her in the dust, while taking her muddy hands in mine to say, "My mother — my mother, it is true. It is all true! Everything we have told you is true! God loves you. Jesus died to save you and He will give you a new life, eternal life."

I still see that old slave woman looking right back at me, struggling to understand things so new, so different, then asking me, "If it is true, why didn't you come before?"

Tears still spring to my eyes. I still hang my head in shame. So many still wait to hear for the first time that Jesus died for them and that they might be freed from the bondage of Satan. Why didn't I come before?

"O Lord Jesus, let someone who reads this book, go quickly, go by prayer, go sacrificially, into the dark places of the world and by faith *'untie some knots in Satan's rope.'"*

www.ingramcontent.com/pod-product-compliance
Lightning Source LLC
Chambersburg PA
CBHW061726070526
44583CB00024B/3017